AUNT PEARL'S
FAMILY REUNION BOOK

Personal Pointers on "How to 'Farley-Up' Your Family Reunion" Reunion Book

JAMES ARRINGTON

DESERET BOOK COMPANY
SALT LAKE CITY, UTAH

To my family &
to your family...
whoever you are

Photographs by Mark Philbrick.
Some of the photographs throughout
the book are courtesy of Future Foods
and also Starpoint Entertainment from
"The Farley Family Reunion" video.

Library of Congress Cataloging-in-Publication Data
  Arrington, James.
      Aunt Pearl's family reunion book : Personal pointers on "How to 'Farley-
up' your family reunion" reunion book / James Arrington.
          ISBN 1-57345-380-3 (pbk.)
          1. Family reunions—Humor.   2. Mormons—Humor.   I. Title.
      PN6162.A685   1998
      818'.5407—dc21   98-16694
                                                                            CIP

Printed in the United States of America

10   9   8   7   6   5   4   3   2   1   72082 - 6375

AUNT PEARL'S
FAMILY REUNION BOOK

JAMES ARRINGTON

CONTENTS

Contents

Leroy, Heber's son

Beatrice

Introduction & Acknowledgments

Aunt Pearl Farley Axelson is a friend of mine, along with family members Uncle Heber, Grampa Dean, Uffer K. Johnson, Aunt Minnie June, Leroy, Tiffany, Vonell, Fayreen and many, many more I've met over the years. When I first became acquainted with the Farleys they changed my life considerably, but I've gotten over that now.

I feel like I've always known the Farleys: they've gone to school with me, lived in my neighborhood, and gone to my church. I met them on my mission, in college, and I even dated several before I met my wife. Then I realized one day that I was related to them, all of them...and you probably are, too.

I'm proud to say that this is a family remarkable in their resilience, startling in their physical resemblances, and astonishing in their incomprehension. As a family they excel at one thing: they hang together, no matter what. Taken as a group, they may be somewhat low on the pecking order of life (though there are Farleys at every level), but they make their place as comfortable, homey, accepting, and worthwhile as they are able. I admire them for that.

When Sheri Dew approached her about writing a book, Aunt Pearl's first words were, "Ohmyheck, Ohmygosh, Ohmyheck . . . Ohmygosh!!"

Introduction & Acknowledgments

It did take some time to convince her that she was fully capable of such a thing. She is grateful to Sheri for having the vision and courage (some would say "the foolishness") to take a chance on this book. Pearl also thanks her designer, Richard Erickson, whose help was invaluable and is obvious on every page of this book; Mark Philbrick for his photographic skills and his ability to take these pictures and not break lenses; and Richard Peterson, her editor, whose grammatical forbearance has been extraordinary. She is also sincerely appreciative of the help she received from Charmaine Stevenson whose assistance with the formulas was critical, and Jennifer Ballard who worked as her research assistant. Dan Thomas, Susan Arrington Madsen, Carl and Chris Arrington, as well as my wife, Lisa, son, Joseph, and daughters, Susanna and Katie Rose, were all understanding and helpful, if not completely demonstrative of the information in this book. Pearl also wishes to thank her original partner, Allison Hickman Warner, and original director, Charles Lynn Frost, for their help, talent, and inspiration over the years.

While you may laugh at this book (and we hope you laugh a lot), I urge you to listen to Aunt Pearl. Her years of experience give her more depth than you might think. We both wish you good luck and good pain reliever on the event of your next family reunion. Oh, and tell all your Farleys "hello" for us.

From left to right: Barley P. Farley our little brother who's got all the money and is V.P. of the family. Heber J. Farley oldest son of 2nd wife, Phoebe, and current President of the Farley Family. Corporation, Organization, Association. Grandpa Asa Dean Farley (seated), the patriotical head of the family. He's holding a picture of Clareance who disappeared in 1970 or so. Above Grandpa is Aunt Minnie June (Farley) Boothe, Granpa's only living sibling. This picture of Priscilla (Insert) was taken on their trip to the islands where she caught Bury-Bury and never recovered. Not a very good picture of Volco Eugene (ex-officio president of the family), but his wife Priscilla sure looks real don't she? Aunt Pearl (Farley) Axelson (Me), Family Treasurer and Historian. This book was wrote by her.

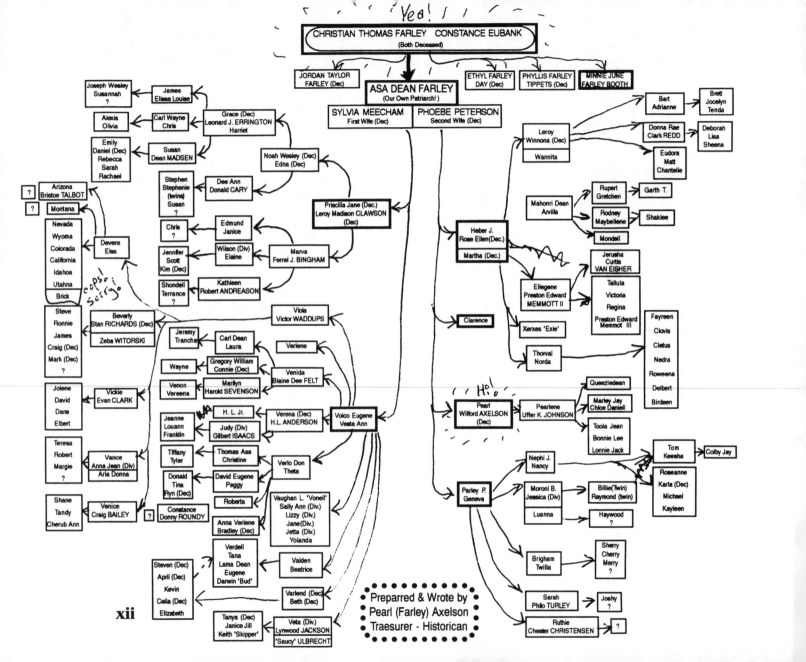

Why I Done This

by Aunt Pearl (Farley) Axelson

As If I Heard a Very Deep Voice . . .

Well, I ain't as young as I used to be. I know that'll come as a shock to some who knows how good I take care of myself, but let me tell you it creeps upon you all unawares. For those as doesn't believe me, you just wait! Anyways, not only that but my body is become my enemy—and those as knows what I mean, knows exactly what I mean. Things going this way, I says to myself, I says, "Pearl, kid, (I always call me "kid") listen here, kid, there's a whole brand new gyration out there that needs the benefits of your knowledge, tuition, and claricity. And it is high-time, as now you got plenty of it, to spend some efforts exposing your posterity and those who otherwise follow along behind you to the light and knowledge to which you have been given."

And, my gosh, it was just as if I heard a very deep voice saying, "You betcha, Pearl, kid, get yourself going!" "Alrighty-dighty, kid," I says to myself, "letter rip!"

And so here I am spending my time relieving pain for others as I have had to relieve it for my very own self over the years, which was at great expense both personally and privately, which I don't want to wish up on any body I know well. I guess thats no secret either! And this is what that relief is spelt like: Family Reunions! And boy can they ever be a pain. Well, its no secret the Farleys has one of the biggest and bestest family reunions ever invented, and with all humblness, that has to do with me. Family Reunions is what I do—its my expertees, so to speak.

SO LISTEN TO AUNT PEARL: Family Reunions doesn't have to be a pain ⚡, but hardly anybody doesn't know that. Here's the problem. You don't want to go and reinvent yourself the wheel! I mean, when I was starting out with family reunions, there wasn't hardly nobody to help me out, was there? How do you organize one? A pretty donting task, huh?

So why don't somebody write up a book as can help? Beats me. Fact, to this day, one of the things I have yet to discover (although I swear I have looked all over heck for it in the stores) is a real easy-to-follow book as which really can truly help you out in FIGURING OUT HOW TO PLAN, PREPARE, AND GET GOING WITH YOUR OWN REAL FAMILY REUNION! (Most especially in a correct and straightforward manner.) Well, you could knock me baldheaded and I'm totally amazed and shocked! When you see how many families there is out there and how few of them know what they're actually doing (and hate it because of it) its just a crying shame, is all.

The year I (Aunt Pearl, me) got stuck up the tree trying to get the kitty (who was already down here).

Oh, alright now, I know there's those books out there that gives it the old college try (whatever that is) to explain it all, and I ain't saying their bad or even close. Its just that I done alot to get where I got and I'd like to leave something behind me which is large towards my posterity as benefits others besides myself. Again, as if I heard a deep voice saying, "Crud, Pearl, get a move on, this is where you can make your counterbution!"

This being the case, now that Wilford left me his spanking new computer, which he never figured out, bless his heart. (Ain't these new-fashioned computers something? I mean, I don't know how they do it, but as I'm going along, it underlines alots of important words—in red no less! Real Patriotical! How does it do that, anyways? But this computer is so dang fun I can change the way words look *see* see **SEE** *see* and even put in little pitchers ☎ ♡ 🐄 🍴 🌐 and everything!)

Anyways, I decided as I would put the some total of my experience down on paper myself, as I know it, so's there won't be anymore mistake and hullbaloo about "how she done this or that" so's you can have the full benefit as to how things really ought to be and so's there all done right and correctly.

And so, here is all the wit and wisdom that has been put through me all these years of these here kinds of things. I put it down into as narrow a book as I could so even I could use it. I have tryed to include plenty of things, thoughts, secret tips, and even some demonstrational sorts of worksheets for how to make your own family reunion—each and every one of them—every bit as good as The Farley Family Reunion at which everybody and there dog  has a good time (and keep you off your sychiatrists couch, too!)

So, here I am, snug as a bug in a rug, Wilford's computer still on Aunt Sis's first sewing machine table (she never did use it much, anyways, as you can tell by her pictures), Postum on the right, and crackers and cheese on the left, to create this magnet opus for you family reunion strugglers across the nations here today and gone tomorrow.

Pearl!

Why? Why Have a Family Reunion Anyways?

Okay, so once upon a time, weigh back when, I was JUST LIKE YOU—I just hated family reunions. Absolutely hated them! Couldn't stand them. Boy, oh, boy, was I sick of them. But, boy, oh, boy, was that a long time ago! I can just hear you saying, "How does she know me like that?!" Well, okay, I ain't sycik (for sure), but much less, it ain't no secret that Family Reunions is become a hiss and a byplane wherever you go. Some families if you can believe it actually go so far as NOT TO HAVE FAMILY REUNIONS just so's that they don't accidentally run into each other. Some people's children! Imagine . . .

But, just think about it for a second or two, don't that just defeat the whole purpose of having a family in the first place? I mean, here's how I got it figured: I figure, no lesser being than the Lord, Hisself, sent you down to your family and you better get used to 'em! Why? I'll tell you why—BECAUSE! ❗

👆 **First of all, A)** The good Lord chose them for you, and what does that say about you?

✌️ **Second, B)** In this world as we have today, your family is your first line of defense much less offense, so bare that in mind.

👌 **Thirdly, C)** If you think staying away from them undoes the work of your gene pools, well, you can just forget that, and, (as if this weren't enough already)—

✋ **Forthly, D)** You can't run away from them by staying away from them because we know families is mighty important to Him who put you in there in the first place. So, that being the case, who do you think you're going to spend your time with in the great here after? (assuming as you go there.) So, if you can't even get onto their level in the here and now, what makes you think the playing field will be level in the there and then? They don't deserve you!

Now, of course, the reasons aren't all really heavy like that. I mean, there's a plenty of really good reasons for holding a family reunion (even if you don't know if you really want to) which I will now write down in a little list for you to tack on your refregerator and ponder:

Check off your faverites: ✔ ✗ ✔ ✗ ✔ ✗ ✔ ✗ ✔ ✗ ✔ ✗ ✔ ✗ ✔ ✗ ✔ ✗

Zerox this here and stick it to your fridge.

- ❏ To find out whose kids are better or worse than yours
- ❏ To get zeroxed everybody else's family history research stuff and get signups to do the exspecially hard ones on yours
- ❏ To have your kids watch how to use the use of personal guilt wherever it is necessary
- ❏ To keep alive family stories, gossip, values, culture, and heritage
- ❏ To brag on your kids to those who needs to know about it
- ❏ To laugh and bawl with those who most understands how come
- ❏ To ask (and give) forgiveness from those who needs it most
- ❏ To mark down who all those people were in the pictures from last year's reunion
- ❏ To have some Kodiak moments (which you can't do when you're a part)
- ❏ To continualizationalize your own peculiar lineage from Adam on down to your kids
- ❏ To get your kids so's they know theirs something more to family than just your own personal branch and twig
- ❏ To push more peace in the world!
- ❏ To see what uncle/aunt/cousin so-and-so has gone off and did with their hair/pants/wait/kids/car this year!
- ❏ And to keep love going and growing in a hostile atmosphere. Cause love at home is the start to love everywhere else!

9

Why? Why Have a Family Reunion?

Now those is some of my best reasons and they are pretty deep, believe you me, but however, I bet YOU got some pretty dang good couple a two or three reasons of your own as you been thinking about it. So, this here is your own personal area to write down your own spacial reasons:

1. _____

2. _____

3. _____

4. _____

SEE THERE?! Isn't that gratifying? And I thought I heard you say you didn't think their was any good reasons to go to the family reunion! Now Zerox this and send it to your kids in college or Dear Abby! Good on ya! Okay, so now that being settled . . .

Chester Christensen,
Ruthies new husband.

Who Pops the Whip?

Ever notice reunions doesn't happen all on their own? Well, heck sakes course not, everybody knows that. I mean, you just don't say, "Okay, let's have one" and one magically appears somehow. That'd be a miracle for sure! BUT . . . (and whenever I put that big "BUT" up there, that means you got to pay extra special attention to my big "BUT" because something very important follows) .

. . BUT somebodies got to take over cause if nobody does, then how will it ever get done, is my question. So, then, who's going to be the top dog, the boss hog, the cats meow. Here's my answer. YOU! if nobody else.

Here's some examples of how you might go about to figure out who is in charge:

➡ My friend Wanda does it every single year or hers would never get done — (Well, I guess not, what with her brothers the way they is and has been.) So she does it. She just grins and bares it as she has for years. Lucky she's good at it and knows how to delegationalize duties as

> **PEARL'S OF WISDOM**
> Whoever's on top is always underneath shoving

needed. This here is a example of the same person organizing it every blessed year. This your basic "BITING THE BULLET" kind of organizing reunion.

➜ My other friend, Taudry's family, does it very different than that. In this next kind, nobody wants the responsibility every single year, so they worked it out on a sort of predestinational-type schedule. Her, being the youngest in their family of thirteen, started it off. It is now working on up to her oldest sister (who I know worked it this way because she'll be passed on before its her turn). I suppose you could also start in the middle and go side to side in an alternator-type fashion. This is the "PERGRESSIVE" or "CHECKOFF" type kind of being in charge.

➤ This next is the way the Farleys does it, and its a very "DEMOCRATICAL" type organization because of the family has to get together and fight about it before they vote on who will carry on the next year. Everybody gets nominated and seconted and voted into their job, lots of times under pressure. But this here is the only way everybody counterbutes and can make a difference. Otherwise, their is always hangers on and "little red henners" who comes and eats and does absolutely nothing else.

➡ Lastly is the "DRAW STRAWS" kind of leadership where you put people in to a hat and draw them out, or I seen them pick cards. I even heard about one family where whoever lost at their family bowling game

was automatically it that next year. Its just the use of some gambling sort of thing to pick the unsuspecting.

➡ Now there is one other way, and that is called the "COMITTEE" approach. I call it the "PHONE BILL" way, on account of what it ends up costing you. This here is where you just have a bunch of people in charge of comittees and they are all supposed to just call each other up and keep things on the straight and narrow. Now this is tricky as who's in charge anyways? Well, don't believe it, cuz one person always winds up doing all the calling and all the rest just winds up doing the receiving. Which means, of course, that you have a president or chairman anyhows and only no body wants to admit it. Not to mention theirs no real way to get all the phone calls paid for except out of your own personal pocket. Aunt Pearl's advise is to beware of this one here.

But now, that does bring us down to comittees (and that's not as far down as you might think).

Comittees

Comittees is absolutely necessary for family reunions to work out. FIRST of all, one person can't do everything even if they want to. (I have personal experiences with this, just ask me.) SECOND, it is a way of getting more people to come, and THIRD, it gives you plenty of people to complain to when things don't go the way you want them to. So comittees is really important for many reasons.

PEARL'S OF WISDOM
Misery needs
company and so do
chairpersons

▼ Picking comittee persons is harder than it sounds as here you can offend people quite a bit without even knowing how. My only help for that is look them straight in the eye and make sure they aren't lying when they tell you they'll do it. So you need a chairperson (pulitically correct!) over each and every single thing, and in fact, the more chairpersons you have the better.

Here is a list of chairpersons as would be pretty useful at your own family reunion:

a. Locations/Reservations
b. Meal coordination
c. Program/Entertainment
d. Games and Activities
e. Meetings
f. Workshops
g. Devotionals (some people really does go overboard)
h. Physical arrangements such as set-up, clean-up, chairs, garbage, and the like. (Don't laugh, you should of seen Terrell's pickup last year out to the park.)

i. Interviews/Blessings from the family patriarch
j. Finances
k. Publicity
l. Registration
m. Memories/Family History
n. Pictures
o. Awards
p. Babysitting coordinator
q. and etc.

You may not think these is all essenshul, but I seen situations where each and everyone of these could've made or broke things. Unfortunately you usually only know if their broke after the fact (which is why I'm warning you in advance). I also know it really looks like its overdoing it (and for some families it will be by quite a ways) to have this many. But here's my rule: The more comittee chairmen you got then the smaller the load on each chairperson, and the smaller the disaster will be when the ball is finally dropped on something! (and something always does).

Here's three mighty good ways you can get these comittees to actually do something for a change.

❶ I call it the "TOP DOWN" organization (and that ain't no convertable, either.) Organize comitties completely by officers of the official family organization, which is made up of such offices such as president, vice president, treasurer, financial secretary, secretary, assistant secretary, business manager, regional coordinator, regional representative, historian, grocer, photographer, and the like. Now you don't have to have all of these, or more correctly, one person can play several hats like I myself am the family genealogist, historican, treasurer, financial secretary, and family verification officer (to expose those as attempted sneaking in last year). All that really means is that I knew what was what, and boy, oh, boy somebody better.

❷ I call it your "GRAB BAG". You put all those things as need to be done in a bag and shake it up and then treat it just like "white elephants." You can either stick with what you draw out, force trade (rob) somebody else for what they got, or you can negotiate different trades for the especially good ones. This way must be done at the family reunion every year. If you break jobs up in to littleler and littleler pieces even kids can partake or even do one of their own. It really is kinda fun (and takes the place of a family game that you don't have to plan for), but you gotta have pertnear everybody there. And no doing it by proxie - Neither! Because if you do it by proxie, all the hardest jobs nobody wants to do all go to the person who isn't there who doesn't give a dang already (cuz where are they?) and so where would you be then? Trust me, that just leads to trouble as we have certainly found out the hard way.

Little Tiffany

❸ "THE PATH OF LEAST RESISTENCE". Family members carry out the same certain assignments each year. This usually happens on its own as some people hate some things and don't mind other things and would rather keep doing the things they don't mind as opposed to what they hate. Like in our family, Twila always does the nametags and hates to cook.

I guess there is other ways of doing all this stuff, but these here is the ways we found is ways that would work.

Whose Supposed to Come?

Now, coarse, I just can't believe anybody actually has to ask this question as it is a oxximormon to say "Who do you invite to a FAMILY reunion?" (WELL, DUH, get it?) But, okay, Theta says as there are probably some of you as ain't been to one, perhaps, or not a good one leastways, whatever, and since this here is meant to be the end all of books for this sort of thing, here is experience on who comes:

❶ For first timers, my advice is just keep it real small. For instance, like only brothers and sisters, or maybe just those as get along and their families. Your going to have a hole heap more trouble doing this then you actually think. It ain't a cakewalk in the park. So, the smaller the easier.

❷ For bigger ones you can do it how we do it. You just pick all the posterity of a certain person—your grampa for instance (even if he's already passed on) since your already related to him. Now on these kinds you can't afford to leave nobody uninvited, no matter what family quarrels are going on, as everybody has a right and nobody has it wrong. Because you certainly wouldn't want to be the starter of a whole new family quarrel, now would you?

❸ Different people for different groups for different kinds of events. Like for instance:

☢ an officers meeting just for planning, damage control, and financial needs

♂ a "Adults Only" meeting (just for peace of mind you might want to plan several of these) and while your busy, you could have—

🚶🚶 a treasure hunt put on by the teenagers for them little ones, which builds family knowledge, unity, and work ethic

🏠 a ladies only breakfast (served by men or kids), or

🚲 an "In-Laws Only" (those that married into your family) for pictures

🏮 maybe even a cartoon room for them kids (more about that later, from Heber), or

🍖 a Saturday BarBee-Q dinner, for everybody and his.

❹ And this one last really important thing on who should come. Sometimes there is somebody really spacial to the family that ain't actually truthfully in the family. You know, like somebody that is sort of "like family," as we used to say. We always used to have Mr. Horton, our milk man, come on a count of so many of us thought he was our father, him being gone so much.

Oh, my heck!! : The Gosh Dang Calendar

There is probly nothing that can get your goat, stick in your craw, and reck your reunion so quick as bad calendarization in the advance planning area. This being the case I have visted over to Arvilla Farley's house who is our nearly perfessional calenderization specialist for the Farley family. Her world of experiences will steer you clear of some real picklish problems so feast here on her perspicacious acumen (thanks to the thesaurus):

PEARL'S OF WISDOM
When to do What
is which to do where
and why!

I am totally grateful for this opportunity to pitch in on Pearl's book. I never wrote one before in all my life. However, I do know something about a budget, and don't you forget it. That's how we got our entire house redone without any extra money.

Keeping the calendar may seem like a teeny-beensy job to some, but I can tell you it takes the headache out of many things, including a family reunion. It's sort of like aspirin for the soul. This is especially true if the family has voted you funds for your telephone solicitation time. Even if they didn't, you cozy up to the treasurer and get the okay for that too, then you can be paid back, and there's nothing illegal about it. But that's another story and one that Pearl will most certainly bring up. (She's very good at cozying!)

DO THIS STUFF WAY AHEAD OF TIME (like a year or so)

Here is NUMBER ONE: Set a date for your reunion at the earliest possible date. Well, what I mean is set it sooner rather than later . . . Uhm, No, no, I mean set it now . . . Heavens to Betsy not NOW, just set it now for in the future! Do you see what I mean?

It is very important to have the date at the earliest possible date so that everybody can plan.

This is NUMBER TWO: This decision should be made with as many people in attendance to discuss it as possible. Also, this decision should not be put off because "so and so" didn't bring their daytimer. Just get everybody as consenting as is possible (which is probably after a helping of Aunt Geneva's Black Forest cake with ice cream). Never try to get a date that is absolutely and completely unanimous or you will never get a date. I told my daughters this exact same advice when they started dating.

> ## Arvilla of Wisdom
> *If you set your standards so high that they can never be reached then they won't be*

> ### PEARL'S OF WISDOM
> Since unanimous dates are impossible – the "next best" date is better any day than a blind date

And when anybody asks you how the heck you came up with this date, here is the reply: "Okay, then, when would YOU suggest it be?!" Honestly, some people are happy enough to let you do all the work, then all they do is complain.

Remembering again that people are always going to be critical of whatever choice you choose for your choice of dates, you need to consider these special considerations:

✓ During summer vacation for your kids sounds easy, but what with year-round schools in lots of places, July is completely eat up with scout camps, youth conferences, family vacations, basketball camps, marching bands, and the like.

✓ In the off-season of a place, when prices are cheaper. Besides, things are not so crowded when a lot of people aren't there.

✓ Holidays are not particularly recommended for the larger type gatherings because of political problems with in-laws and the like.

✓ Anniversaries, weddings, graduations, or other major individual family events are dangerous because for sure these overshadow the depth and breadth of the family reunion for those they are happening to.

✓ Making a certain time each year (such as a second weekend in August) is made to be broken, but it always brings up important things and sometimes is smarter to start off with.

✓ And, lastly but certainly not leastly — do it when MOST people say that they can commit to coming. I say MOST people because that is exactly what I mean. If you think all people can come on the day you select even under a vote, then you got another think coming! There is no hope to being unanimous, as has already been mentioned.

Use these lines for your personal best guess about when would be good for you.

day   month   year
_____/_____/_____
_____/_____/_____
_____/_____/_____

(STOP) ACTION POINT: This is a REALLY extremely important step! If there's no date, then there'll be no reunion. And if people can't plan in advance . . . well, they can't plan in advance. So, put some starch in your spine and write down on this line when your next family reunion is going to be. Stop and call if you haven't got it decided yet. Don't write nothing down at all till you have got it — decided, I mean.

day   month   year
_____/_____/_____

THERE NOW, SEE! YOU GOT A TARGET DATE! AND THAT'S A DECISION TO BE PROUD OF AS IT WILL BE THE FIRST ONE YOU EVER PLANNED... WITH ARVILLA'S HELP, SUCCESS IS GUARANTEED!

Since it'll never be unanimous you better pick it, plan on it, and just go with common (and Pearl's) consentuals which is a principle of American Law too. If nobody else will pick the date, then you get your first choice. Neat, huh?

From here on out now your job is now to become Mr (or Mrs. or Miss)

(P.S. [That stands for "Pearl Says." This will be my little way of helping when there needs to be a note since Arvilla never wrote a book before.] A date can be changed if it has to come down to it, but if you don't have something to change FROM then your pretty well cooked anyway, right? It's like saying I think I'll change my dress when your wearing a pantsuit. You see what I mean? Mark it down—the date—than hang onto it like superglue. The people who is always wanting to change the date probably wouldn't show up anyway. That's been my experience, and I guess I've had a little.)

23

BIG BEN

(p.s. For those who doesn't know, Big Ben is a large clock back in England that REMINDS everybody what time to hold to.)

And if, perchance, you don't think of reminding as important, let ME remind YOU that reminding is as old as the hills and twice as dusty. Wasn't it Adam who said to Eve, "Don't you remember we weren't supposed to eat that?" So, reminding is good (unless it's after the fact; then it just turns to nagging). Okay, here is the first reminder for you, the Reminder —

- Get and keep a list of all Committee Heads for the purpose of communications. I swear you will never regret this move, I promise you, scouts honor. Even though it's the President or the Chairman that should be doing all this, just remember, who will remind them?! Well, it turns out that the calendar person is that very person. (Remember, you are the timing chain of the whole bottle of wax!)

Here's some other reminders of who to remind about what, when:

✓ Remind all Committee Heads that they are heads of committees with all that entails.

✓ Remind the Treasurer and all the Committee Heads to set up their budgets early. I guess this is pretty obvious on paper, but it isn't off. (p.s. This usually saves on some money as this can cost time, money, and really very poor behavior later on when people find out it ain't how they thought.)

✓ Remind the Reservations Committee to make them way in advance (for camping, boating, cabins, or whatever else).

✓ Remind the Registration Committee and/or Publicity Committee and/or Secretary about

24

locating missing family members (especially those you can't find). The reason they are lost in the first place is because somebody didn't remind them to keep in touch.

OKAY THEN, NEXT UP. . . .

WITH YOUR REUNION DATE ALREADY CAST DOWN TO CEMENT ALL YOU DO IS BACK IT UP THREE MONTHS (or add nine months if you're more than a year in advance) TO COME UP WITH THAT FATEFUL DAY THREE MONTHS BEFORE YOU ACTUALLY ARE GOING TO HAVE YOUR NEXT REUNION – Write it down here _____/_____/_____.

Whew! Okay, that being done . . . (and don't deceive yourself on this) now you can get going on about your life normally and naturally – if this is really done and finished as you say it is. Don't worry too much now and expose yourself to the finer things of life. Things will get tough later on so reward yourself now so you have something to look back on.

Write down here "some pleasant plans I have" for this nine months:

_____

_____

_____

_____

Then comes that fate filled day . . .

THREE MONTHS BEFORE, but Don't Panic

Okay, it isn't the "Battle of the Bulge" yet - which I might add, me and Pearl fight all the time, but things are getting close enough to start looking at things in a very much closer manner. Follow these directions closely:

(p.s. speak for yourself, Arvilla)

✓ Get the Chairman or President to get them committees completely committed! (this serves as a real good reminder with plenty of time left to fix what hasn't been done yet).

✓ Reminders should go to all committee chairmans or whoever is in charge of (this is double checking especially if your President is as forgetful as ours is) such as the

✓ Activities Committee, Program Committee, and for sure for sure the Attendance Committee,

‒ or ‒

from each and every different chairman (with a special eye on the lackadaisical kind)

✓ Remind the Publicity Committee to get a move on! (p.s. This is most spacially important because if nobody doesn't know about it, then it ain't going to be such a great reunion, anyhow, is it?)

✓ Now's the time to double-check the reservations and cross-check them with the Attendance Committee (saves a ton of worry).

✓ Each and every chairperson should check on committee member assignments. This way delegation has half a chance to work. Remind them to say "uh-huh" and "good idea" and

26

"sounds good" a lot since the assignment person is probably thinking about this for the first time and is making it up on the phone as they go. (p.s. If they aren't just making it up they'll be offended if you quarrel with there ideas anyhow! So keep it positive.)

✓ Send out final registration information (it won't do any good, actually, but it's a dang good reminder) (p.s. If they aren't just making it up they'll be offended if you quarrel with there ideas anyhow! So keep it positive.)

✓ Collect money (and this is really sure to take lots of effort . . . ask me, I know).

✓ And, finally, get the "FINAL HEAD-COUNT." Just a wise word to the wise, this is only just what you call it, not what it really is. (p.s. What Arvilla means is things is for sure going to change till the very moment your supposed to reunionize and then some! This happens every year so its nothing to worry about unless its the people who's house your all going to. Now, that can be a real let down!)

WITHIN A MONTH OF THE REUNION? YIPES!

✓ Triple-check the Reservations Committee and cross-check with the Attendance Committee – sometimes they are one and the same.

✓ Triple-check all committee assignments (to see what you have to fix that wasn't). Send out your "FINAL NOTICE" flyers with details on when (you cannot believe how many people cannot remember since yesterday!) and where the reunion is AND with

✓ a map. (p.s. draw the map on the back. If it's attached separately it could get just as lost as they will looking for the reunion. Plenty of relatives can follow a map but can't read directions – I think it has something to do with Boy Scouts!).

27

Also include with this any "last minute changes" or other important information (such as "Remember, $5.00 fee for park entrance," or "Wally, you owe 72 dollars for pictures from last year and can't eat until it's paid up" sorts of things or whatever).

With these little reminders over the months you can sit back and say "I done it" with perfect assurity. Thanks to everybody and good luck.

Arvilla Farley

My extensive thanks to Arvilla for this perfectly important and weigh functional information. I actually learned some stuff as I didn't even know by sitting down with Arvilla! Shows to go ya! So that's what she's been up to all these years. Pretty sneaky. Well you can bet that if you was to take these advises it'll save you a ton of worry right along with several other things and some money along with! Pearl

(P.S. Warning! Do not vent your spleen on this little reminder area to much, as it can be a great turn off and then people won't come and then you'll NEVER get paid your money!)

28

Where in Heck Is Your Reunion to Be?

This topic is probably one of the ones that causes more contension even hypertension onto every family than any other excepting money. Trying to get family members to agree on a place to hold it is like trying to get a family picture with everybody smiling, all there eyes open, and no devils fingers! Fat chance!

One reason why this is sure to be one of the biggest headaches there is is because families with teenagers always likes lakes and families with little kids is a scared of them and visa versa. So, there needs to be tolerance here, and always in the vein of safety. Here is some ideas for your consideration so's you don't have to go and reinvent yourself the wheel since it was already on the bike already. Some things to think about with regards to this:

★ Is there some memory or thing you're trying to remember, celebrate, or inibriate—like your old school, or your birthplace, or your old dogs grave, or the site of the old family homestead, or some such?
(write one or two)_____

✳ Most families has it in the hometown where most of there family is buried. Where's that? (write)_____ Problems: the people who live there don't just bring everything to a screeching halt to meet with the other members who've put out considerable to arrive. This can cause frixation.

☆ Others have it in the hometown of the most well to do family (especially if you want to use their house) who's that?
(write)_____or,

✳ I know some as holds it in the hometown of the poorest family so's they don't have to travel as expense. (Don't write this down as that might give offense, but we know who we're talking about, correct? And there's one more idea here—

PEARL'S OF WISDOM

A change is as good as a vacation so visit your family for a change

★ Hold it in the town of the people who never come
. . . that way they got no excuses at all. This here is a diller of an idea but approach it real delicate! (Don't write this down neither, but its obvious who.)

Lots of this, of course depends on the size of your reunion and the number of living in your familes. Just remember this isn't a vacation exactly, but only sort of like one.

You have other times you can go other places so this one shouldn't be only for just fun (which it always is sure to be because of old uncle whats-his-name that shows up every year with his latest invention, girl-friend, horse, belt buckle, or what have you. Now that's fun!).

As to what actual place to hold it, here are some ideas I seen tried by us and others:

A park, a beach, a family farm, a desert, a ocean, a campground, a football field, a new (or old) construction sight, a quarry, a lake, a mountain side, a golf course, a hill or vale (or other outdoor arena for larger reunion type activities), a stream, a small river, a big river, a huge river, a small island (remember the safety factor), a resort, a swimming resort, a national park, a rodeo, a restaurant, or hotel for smaller or spacial reunions (most expecially if you know somebody who owns one of these here and can cut you a good deal).

Once these kinds of decisions is reached then consider this following checklist for you to actually truly help you decide FOR REAL WHERE:

1. In some ways where you hold it depends on how much money you got. How much have you got? (write)_____ .

2. Is this a real true budget or is this dreaming? _____,_____
yes   or   no

3. How much do you want to spend? (or better, how much do you think your people will actually pay to go to this place?) _____

4. Now divide it amongst the families and people involved: Budget ÷ payers = _____. Is that a reasonable cost? (remembering, of course, that what is reasonable to you sure isn't to somebody else related to you.)

_____,_____
yes   or   no

If its a "no go" or guaranteed to make lots of "no shows," better pack it in and try this:

1. Who's place was it had at last year? (write) _____

2. How long did they say it took to recover? (write) _____

3. Will they even have you back again? _____,_____(hint: how was the house and property left when you left?) yes or no

4. Would you ever WANT to go back again? _____,_____
yes   or   no

5. If that don't work, who else would risk it? _____, or_____ or _____. (You can only try 'em and see, and you might use a little admiration like, "But we never been to

your house before and everbody wants to see it."
If you don't lay it on too thick, that kind of talk
can go a long ways towards making the deal.) ➤

PEARL'S OF WISDOM
Vinegar never
attracted a bee
so don't you start

If your paying attention here you'll notice
I'm talking about people's home towns not
cabins or campgrounds or the like. Nutral
sights like those are just as good BUT (a very
big BUT), remember usually **more expensive**.

After all this, use these lines to write down
your three favorite choices:

1. _____
2. _____
3. _____

For the 10 Bestest Places where the Farley Family goes turn ☞ yourself over to page __91__

How Long Should Your Reunion Be?

Thats an easy one: As long as you can stand it. And that could be

• As little as one single meal, or

• As many as three days to a week (but really probly not more, if you want peace)

Considerations to consider:

The traveling distance of family members—the farther they live away, the longer the reunion should probably be to make it worth it. (Of course this has a limit—when Gretchen came all the way from Germany we still only had it on a afternoon, a night, and a morning. It might have been different if her husband Rupert who was the actual member of the family had come with.)

How Do I Get a Hold of Family Members?

This here, of course, certainly depends on how big your reunion is going to be and how big you'd like to actually get it to be. ➡

If its so big that you have to actually track people down that you or

PEARL'S OF WISDOM
Reunions:
The bigger they is
The harder they is

some member of the family who is close to you don't know them, then your not planning a family reunion but a symposium or a seminary or something, and I don't have to tell you how those can be . . .

BUT just in case your planning **REALLY BIG**, here is some ideas:

• Send mailers to each heads of family (siblings or others); let them pass on information to their own children, grandchildren, cousins, and in-laws, etc. (saves postage)

• Keep a record file for larger families or make a directory to be updated each reunion (you will definately want a separeate secretary, committee, or some other to handle this deal)

• Send out a "Missing Persons" ad with every mailer (you could even offer a funny or cute reward like Eunice give. A free kitten. I got plenty to give too . . .)

• Make a round-robin newsletter between reunions, and

• This is strange, but my friend Relda actually took out a ad in the newspaper and found her nephew Elwood, much to their surprize and a shocker for the family, too! (She used the idea of a will being found with money in it . . . she is such a kill!)

Uffer K. Johnson, husband to Pearlene, Pearl's daughter.

$$\$\$$ THE Budget $\$\$$

Okay, Here's (yikes!!!)

Where the rubber meets the pavement . . .

where the brass hits the tack . . .

and where theirs egg on the bread or on your face!

This here part of the family reunion is the totally most important part, the sumoom bonum, the alfalfa and omega, and where the buck stops (get it?). You, being who you are, of course think that family reunions is about relationships and crying and laughing together, taking pictures for posterity, and all that. Your absolutely right. BUT without this here money part to grease the works, let me just tell you, this machinery ain't going nowhere, and fast!

This here is the part where my personal migraine always used to start and end. I have had to rely almost entirely over the years on intuition and luck in working on this family budget as nobody else (at least nobody with any smarts) would touch it with a ten foot pole or lived too

PEARL'S OF WISDOM

Of the many affairs in a family both private and un, money is the one as really takes the cake

far away. Finally I went down to Arvilla's place and says, "Lookee here, this is driving me up the tree, could you help me make a defined way to figure this all out so I'm not in bed with the heber jeebers after the whole thing is done?" And we have did it! Thank heavens! I do think inspiration to our relations worked through as we done this. If there is a worse part to the family reunion than the budget, I don't know what it is that really brings this out.

So, me and Arvilla worked out these scientific-type "FORMULAS"—her with the mathematicals and me with the practicals. BIG HINT: If you do your sums in the order in which there in, your sure to come out right (or about as right as you can get) with your own family budget.

Okay, How Do We Handle the Wallet?

This is always a ticklish issue as most everybody would like someone else to pay for things since there never sure there coming until they come. But you gotta be tough on this.

To save yourself a Tylenol month or two (and probly high blood pressure to boot) remember these things:

1. IT IS EASIER ON YOU TO GIVE BACK THAN COLLECT

• so start to collect funds early

• make a plan for money and stick to it, so much per month into the kitty

- or -

• gather money for your next reunion at your current reunion (which is almost impossible because they already spent it getting to this one)

- or -

PEARL'S OF WISDOM
You can't operate without a anesethesia and you can't have a barrel of fun without cash on the barrelhead

• get family dues, donations, registration fees up front. Some people I know charged little penalties (like credit cards do) for being late (LATE FEES) but that just made everybody mad and they wouldn't pay the penalties. Much better, charge them less money up front like a discount for paying early. This takes some planning out, in advance, but you don't want to do this at all if you can't plan out, in advance, let me tell you!

2. SAVE $$$$$ WHERE POSSIBLE!

First off, everybody will just love you for this. Really—but only if they know. So you got to explain it to them first how you done it or they'll never know. However, the distinct problem is that if you save money they

PEARL'S OF WISDOM
Frugality is next
to cleanliness in you
know where . . .

will put you in charge of it again next year. So keep that in mind, too. (Hint: This is definately the door out if you've just had it.) Here's some money **SAVING** suggestions:

• send out mailers along with your Christmas, Valentine, birthday, or round-robin greeting cards

• use your own family talents, cooks, four wheelers, houses, games, horses, and other things rather than rent them.

LaDawncha (most names in our family is pretty normal, but LaDawncha was named after her mother, father, and a Indian friend), LaDawncha always says to me, **"Comparison Shop, Comparison Shop,"** which I think is fine, except for one thing—to be perfectly honest I can't find one! I hear about them all the time, but I've tried to look it up in the yellow pages numerous times and cannot find the address. If you know where one is please send me the address as it appears to be a fantastic place for bargains.

3. CREATE YOUR BUDGET UP FRONT AND PERSONAL

There's a couple of things about reunions that nobody ever actually gets correctly and one of them is this one here. Of course there is a million ways to do this. Some people actually uses the reunion budget to settle up old scores and things like that (which isn't bad so long as both sides knows its going on and AGREES to it up front).

4. MAKE SOME MONEY (FOR THE FAMILY!) IF YOU CAN

PEARL'S OF WISDOM
Preplanning actually comes before planning and planning comes before spending. Don't get them out of order, or else!

Now I know there is some unscrupulus persons out there whoer gonna read this and say to themself, "Goll, hey, I could make some extra cash on this reunion this way!" Yeah, sure. Just two things to think about about this.

☠ A.) If you was to make any money you better plan to take the secret of it with you to the grave and hide your tracks every year—even if you only do it once. If anybody else in the family ever finds out you fleeced them this way then you and your wife AND kids are dead meat (even if they didn't know about it).

☠ B.) If your families anything like mine they are so tight they won't give you the opportunity to make a prophet on anything in general or specific. If there's a way to save it, that's what they'll do and then what'll ya do with all that extra stuff in your garage?

41

Here's the way it really is:

Budget Realities

☛ It probly sounds rotten, but think about it. On your first one maybe just try to break even, then aim for profit later to invest back in for the next time.

☞ Have a fundraiser (one time or ongoing):
- sell family merchandise (with name, crest, logo on them)
- have a family store (with merchandise contributed by all members, like a garage sale sort of. Just beware of some families who'll try to dump all there entire DI stuff or garbage on you)
- create a memory book, photo album, video, etc. for sale to family members (at a slightly higher price)
- hold a auction, raffle, or lottery (but be careful of your state laws and TAXES)

☛ We'd never get away with it, but my friend Donelle's family actually charges admission for small kids (to pay for baby sitting etc.)

☛ Put away a monthly fee into savings so it'll grow during the year (better assign a separate chair person or secretary to keep track or someone for sure will say they paid when they didn't. (You always hate to have to get down to "proofs".)

The "Formulas"

Now don't get nervous. If the word "formula" sounds all scarey like ninth grade math (Remember Mr. Sternup? Yipes!) then just think of it as what you feed your baby. . . and if you don't feed that to your baby (but the other) just realize what I said here.

Since never the same amount of people come that says there going to (or not, as the case may be), here is the "formula" for figuring out how many people will ACTUALLY show up on the day of the reunion. This is an important number for advance planning. (Its pretty simple but more intelligent than it might look at first look):

Actual Attendence "Formula"

Start with the total actual numbers of the family who actually agreed or maybe agreed to come. This is "those coming or who SAYS their coming." _____ (keep a running total on these numbers—and if you don't want to write in the book, just zerox it out and do it separate like.)

COMING (A) _____

Of (A) 8.6% will have big job changes, so SUBTRACT that number (8.6% of A) from A to get B _____

Of (A) 5.4% will be ill, so SUBTRACT that number (5.4% of A) from B to get C _____

Of (A) 5.2% will be pregnant, so SUBTRACT that number (5.2% of A) from C to get D _____

Of (A) 2% will die, so SUBTRACT that number (2% of A) from D to get E _____

Of (A) 19% will have a marriage (which costs so much the whole family won't show up this year unless the groom or bride is ritzy), so SUBTRACT that number (19% of A) from E to get F _____

Of (A) 6% will go on missions or into the Peach Core, so SUBTRACT that number (6% of A) from F to get G _____

continued onto next page please

Of (A) 4.9% will have summer marching band practice or some such, so SUBTRACT that number (4.9% of A) from G to get H _____

Of (A) 11% will have their car break down, so SUBTRACT that number (11% of A) from H to get I _____

Of (A) 21% is what we call our "wild card" no-shows, which includes those in jail, military service, divorce court, or who will be hit with tax liens, unexpected pregnancy, nervous breakdowns, sudden peoplephobia, emergency surgery, marital strife, or the like, so SUBTRACT that number (21% of A) from I to get J _____

Of (A) 18% will change their minds not to come, so SUBTRACT that number (18% of A) from J to get K _____

This here is the SUBTOTAL of those that **was** coming that now aren't coming after all: (K) _____

Compare this (K) to (A)! Makes you think, huh? Caution: Now don't push the panic bell as this figure nearly always is really low, sometimes really, really low. But don't worry cause the next section bucks her back up there again real quick:

Of (K) 14% of them will change there mind back, so ADD that number (14% of K) to K to get L _____

Of (K) 22% that didn't sign up decide to after all, so ADD that number (22% of K) to L to get M _____

Of (K) 1.9% will change jobs and move closer, so ADD that number (1.9% of K) to M to get N _____

Of (K) 4.2% will marry and bring their partner (this also includes adoptions and them step-kids areas), so ADD that number (4.2% of K) to N to get O _____

Of (K) 4% will return from missions etc. , so ADD that number (4% of K) to O to get P _____

Of (K) 7.9% will be mothers bringing one or more new kids, so ADD that number (7.9% of K) to P to get Q _____

Of (K) 11% will bring friends (boyfriends, girlfriends and others), so ADD that number (11% of K) to Q to get R _____

And of (K) 5% will turn out to be neighbors helping, or entertainment, or some such, so ADD that number (5% of K) to R to get S _____

This here then is the TOTAL NUMBER WHO WILL ACTUALLY SHOW UP. (S) _____

don't go and forget this number

There you go! Easy as pie! And simple too. Of all those who will finally figure out the way to get to the family reunion (S)!!!!! is the number. **Now don't go and lose this number.**

I once taught all this to my friend Nona from Moa—who married Noah from Loa—(I just love to say that, sounds Polynesian, don't it!) Anyway, she said, "Where did you get all these complicated figures to multiply with, Pearl?" And I says to her (probably with a pained expression on my face), I says, "Experience and a whole lots of years trying it out." The truth is, I don't know why it works. Who can understand such things? That's the beauty of it. And that's my answer to you as well. Of course, your family might be different, ours certainly is. That being the case you may have to adjust these figures or (heaven forbid) make up your own. GOOD LUCK is all I got to say!

The Food "Formula"

Once you got that number ("S"– have you lost it yet?) under your belt then your ready to tackle **THE FOOD BUDGET**. I personally think the food budget is really the worstest part to figure out. It just drives me crazy and gives me hives and the headache besides, exspecially being as since I ain't naturally blessed with this kind of talent as Arvilla is. But I've learned as I've went. So, here's for how we figure food. (This is only for homecooked type food as restraunt food can vary widely, as you no doubt already know.)

you're allmost there

47

To arrive at a real true GRAND TOTAL number we broke it down into four littleler or "sub" "formulas" which we then added together for the total GRAND TOTAL:

a. The soda pop "formula"

This gives people such fits that some makes everybody bring there own. Now I ain't against that necessarilly, but when I got a good "formula" there ain't much to worry and fret about.

All you do is you take "S"(remember S?) _____

and TIMES it by the number of days (1/2 days is acceptable) x _____
in the reunion = _____

TIMES that against the average temperature (in celsius)
during that time of the year x _____ = _____

then DIVIDE that by the CURRENT cost of a sixpack (of pop)
at your local pop place ÷_____ = _____

now TIMES that by the total percentage of abstainers from
pop (meaning 5.2 % pregnant, 4% is infants, 8% is athletes
"in training," 6% are abstainers for concious, 5.4% are
elderly and don't drink it making a total of 28.6%) x _28.6%_

and that equals THE POP/SODA "SUB TOTAL" OF _____
SERVINGS (cans)

Which you then go down and buy at the grocery store. Here's a hint: make sure you get their store brand, which is generally cheaper by half than those other kinds (and if you buy it in two leeder bottles, its even cheaper than that—see "Making Money," p. ~~41 48 47~~ page 41

See now? This isn't so bad, is it? In fact, it even gets to be sort of fun, huh? except for this next . . .

Okay, it is finally here, the deamon of the whole dang thing. Luckily, with our tried and true "formula" you got no problems here anymore although I got to admit as thinking about it makes me break out in a sweat still.

b. The ACTUAL food "formula"

First, you got to figure out on how many meals your going to have together. In our family we usually go for a lunch (on arrival day), a dinner (that night), a breakfast (the next morning), another lunch (that next day), another dinner (that next night) and that's it for us. This is how you can calculate yours: Count all the Number of Meals _____
TIMES the number of eaters _____

WAIT! How do you figure the number of eaters?! Easy! SUBTRACT those as will have half portions like those as doesn't like the choice, is sick from yesterdays travel or food, or ain't breakfast-type folks, etc.

49

Next you have to ADD back in those as will double portions like teenagers, atheletes, Ferrell and his brothers (I bet you have some like him—he really likes to eat everybody out of house and home—particularly at the family reunion)

Next up you got to figure in those with special needs like DIABETES, NURSING MOTHERS, VEGETARIANS, SALTLESS EATERS, NURSING KIDS, etc. and other such prevelant eating disorders. These will need special attention.

This now makes **116%** of eaters you got to feed. Strange isn't it?

However, don't gripe about this as hardly nobody eats every dang meal even if their hungry. For instance, only **50%** of the people comes by the time of the first lunch no matter what they say.

10% still hasn't arrived by dinner time the first night. (means only cooking for 106%!)

15% don't get up or hate breakfast on the first morning, (so that's down to 101%) but look out because, including moochers, approximately **125%** will eat the Lunch the next big day (including the **116%** from above).

This percentage drops to **88%** that night at dinner when some people is sick and/or leaves. Then if anyone is left the next morning, they are OYO ("ON YOUR OWN.") I don't know how you do it. But that's how we do it.

"So, now wait, Pearl" your saying, "just how do you turn this into a budget for my use?" Okay, now don't you worry because we're finally here at the easy part:

1. FOR BREAKFASTS: MULTIPLY your breakfasts by 57 cents, (the breakfast cost) for each eater (which, if you remember in this case is 101%).
(S) _____ x 101% (1.01) x .57 = _____

And that's budget for that breakfast! Maybe your family likes a heavy breakfast. If it gets up around $1.99 per eater just go to Dennys—no fuss no muss!

2. FOR LUNCH (the first day): MULTIPLY the cost of $1.00 per eater with 50% of which is the total that will come to that first lunch.
(S) _____ x 50% x $1.00 = _____

Now, I know what your thinking. Your saying, "Pearl, scrud this here is starting to look like algebra!?" I know it. But it ain't, so quit your worrying, besides if it was I just give you all the cheats! Think about that for a sec.

3. FOR DINNER: Simple! You figure the cost at $2.50 per eater and TIMES that towards the percentage of the figure of "S."
(S) _____ x 106% x $2.50 = _____

Do this for all your meals based on the percenteeges you found on page 50 (or your own percenteeges if your family is different).

Once you've did all of this, all you do is add all the individual meals up and you'll arrive at a very clean number for the

Total FOOD "SUB TOTAL" _____

c. The snack/dessert "formula"

This includes chips, dip, candy, cake, pie, cookies, nuts, pretzels, pickled eggs, beef sticks, taffy, bagels, veggie trays, cheese and crackers, them little smokie wieners, pork rinds, onion rings, pickles, salsa, and the like. (Don't it set your mouth watering?) This formula is as easy as falling off a beef truck.

> (S) TIMES four desserts _____
>
> TIMES 5 snack periods (namely, between lunch and dinner, between dinner and bed, between breakfast and lunch, between the next lunch and the next dinner, and between that and bed) _____
>
> TIMES 12 cents (the cost of one packet of Alka Seltzer) plus a pack of Alka Seltzer, one for each person.
>
> This here, then, is your snack/dessert budget Total "SUB" TOTAL _____

(By the way, this does not include the one thing every family brings as snacks for themselves. Better add in $5 dollars more per each family who won't honestly have the common courtesy to bring a snack for everybody else.)

d. Plastics/paper "formula" (dishes, utinsuls, etc.)

Alright, I know this category is not food! BUT, heck, we're talking about napkins, plates, bowls, knifes and forks and spoons, cups, plastic bowls, and paper towels which is all absolutely necessary for your food. So, unless you got somebody like Arvilla in your family, who takes a lot of these home and washes them for the next year, you better plan on most of this going straight into the trash. Its definitely a big part of the cost of things and has to be figgered in unless, of course, you would like to donate it from your own personal checkbook? So here's the formula:

Take 10% of the TOTAL of the FOOD SUB TOTAL
and POP and SNACKS) _____

TIMES the number of days of the reunion _____

DIVIDED BY the total sum of infants
and deaths in the family this year.
And there ya go

Total of plastics/paper "formula" "SUB" TOTAL _____

Now, your done except for one particular thing. If your up for the Grand Fetching Total then you better sit down to do this:

ADD UP the TOTAL FOOD SUB TOTAL and the POP SUB TOTAL and the SNACK SUB TOTAL and the PAPER SUB TOTAL for the Total TOTAL of the GRAND Total FOOD TOTAL. Write it here _____

And there you got it—the most painless (and I know it ain't totaly painless) possible way there is to get it, and you got it. Congrats!

/// WARNING ///

TO EVERYBODY: These TOTAL costs should only really represent things that everybody AGREES to pay for together or there will be "you know what" to pay (which sometimes is a heckuva problem all by itself—but I leave that up to you and your own personal close family to fix).

Some families for just one instance, pays for their own personal food bills instead of eating the kitty. If everybody is supposed to bring there own food, and some doesn't that can also lead to problems. (Like in our family, cousin Orville used to always show up to our house without bringing nothing to eat and stands around looking all gaunt and hungry while were having dinner. If it was just him, it wouldn't be so bad, but looking at his little kids, I could just bawl. That's why I think its good to always bring a little extra.)

Others will have a HIRED cook (who is either in or out of the family) and, of course, theirs groceries to buy plus the cook to pay (but that's the way alot of people, especially the ladies, likes it up to the family reunion).

Then again, others will have a catered affair. Things like that make me blush, but it depends totally on what kind of family you got. Maybe you don't even know what you got yet . . . pay attention. This here thing is important because they cost you (and everybody else) money!

Lodging or Bed "Formula"

PEARL'S OF WISDOM
The difference between a cheap bed and a expensive bed is mostly the cost

This will seem quite the unimportant deal to most—exspecially if they ain't been down this long lonesome highway once or twice. But the problem with this here is that the problems and difficulties here only show up once everybody is already tired from travel or the daily reunionizing and tempers has become short and perhaps beds and budgets as well. So it behooves you to treat this serious-like and make certain you aren't caught up all underwears.

Write down the number of sleepable homes (those that are close enough to drive to and are willing to put up with cousins) in the area you've chose _____

TIMES this by the number of available toilets in these houses

x_____ = _____

ADD ONTO it the number of children _____

continued onto next page please

Then DIVIDE this number by the number of children _____

Then TIMES this by 16% (which is a little more than once and
a half the percentage of tithing). This equals the number
of private sleeping spaces (BUT NOT BEDS) you will need _____

TIMES that number by the cheapest rate of rooms you can hunt down
in the city where your having the reunion (or even a nearby town if it
ain't too much of a drive for the savings. (Example: $29.95 at Motel 6.)

This will give you The Lodging Budget TOTAL _____

PEARL'S OF WISDOM

Sometimes a "lost and
found" turns to a "came
and went" and then to a
"washt I hadn'ta"

Lost Articles Mailback "Formula"

There's no doubt but what this is probly a brand
spanking new consideration for most folks. But let me
tell you, one year at our place alone the mail backs in
our personal family cost over seventy-five dollars as
we can count (and which was never paid back for by
the families involved except one) and guess who's
pocket it come out of? Well, don't set me to boiling
here as I'd like to keep some kind of good feeling in
this regard. But that cost don't even reflect or count

or show the cost of long distance calls from both ends or the wasted gas going different places looking for things, as much less the time actually involved in worry and bother. So listen to Aunt Pearl on this because its a true thing!

PEARL'S OF WISDOM
Finders weepers
Just might keepers

Okay, so you can now see I hope this could be something important to work hard on. It saves money and agravation and it also creates a up front kind of interest in people taking care of their own belongings and things, like a reminder or a sort of threat.

Take the number of children _____

TIMES the number of days in the reunion _____

DIVIDE this number by the number of days it took the Lord to build the earth (6, for those as don't know their creation from Adam). This will give you the average number of things lost and write it here _____

DIVIDE this number by the number of families that drove or come in from out of town _____

continued onto next page please

That right there, as staggering as it appears, is the number of mailings you'll have to do. TIMES that number by $2.50 average which is the normal cost of the post down to the post office This will give you the Total Cost to mail lost articles back to their rightful owners

Lost Articles Mailback TOTAL_____

(p.s. I forgot, there is another shortcut to this mailback formula but its not quite so accurut. It is 2 TIMES the % of lactating mothers in the family TIMES 10% of your Desserts and Snacks Budget.)

However, you can eliminate all this bother if you make a box and label it "Lost and Found" and keep it till the next year. One little word of warning on this point though: All that kids stuff will be out of size plus fashion, don't ya know, in a whole year from now. And your going to have to be pretty dang tough to hold peoples stuff back (which is rightfully their own even though they left it) that long a time without some personal feelings getting hurt and their dander up. So you might as well get yourself a fund to take care of this since it is real and I never been to a reunion yet where people didn't discover they couldn't live without something they left behind.

Meal Planning Tips

(I wanted to insert this here somewheres, since I can't see anywhere's else to do it, this is where I'll do it. I took some real good notes when I went down to the Education Week. Or was it the Youth Conference planning meeting down to the stake? Never mind, here they are):

Potluck Dinners

These here cuts down on up front costs from everybodies collective wallet, but your still paying to make it in the first place (like at the churchhouse dinners). One trouble is sometimes the various dishes don't arrive in very good shape. (Like one year when my Potatoes au Gratin arrived as Potatoes Hog Rotten, all over the passenger side of my Pinto (thanks to a crazy driver on the freeway - Thanks alot, I'm sure!) So, sometimes they spills on the trip to the reunion. Oh, and I remember when red Tropecle punch (!) leaked all over Genevas new husbands cars carpet—its still there too. Still, these potlucks can be a cost and labor-saving device so consider it. Here's some guidelines:

Encourage family members to bring family "specialties." This can be chancy though because to be truthful, some people's specialties are not all that well liked. (I don't know why Utahna every blessid year brings that zuccuni and egg plant casserole of hers. Heber, bless his heart, always tries to be a good sport and get a little down, but he's the only one, and he told me last year he didn't think he could do it anymore, sorry, Utahna).

Have various people use recipes from a family cookbook (when we get one . . . hint, hint, Heber).

Organize categories of foods for different branches of the family—salads, main dishes, desserts, beverages, breads, fruits and vegetables, ice, paper goods, condiments (NOTE: this is just a orgunizational nightmare, but if you can do it "good on ya!").

Assign out-of-towners items that can be purchased locally. (Only this raises cries of "favertism" and "unfair burdening" practices so beware of this one.)

Have family members bring side dishes and desserts while paying for the main course, paper goods, and condiments, which would be provided at the reunion. (Just which pocket do you want to pay your bill from, the family kitty or your own pocket when you get there?)

Have them bring their own meat and one additional item. (This is good only for smaller reunions I think. I mean, imagine bringing enough meat for one Farley family and trying to keep track of it through the whole reunion - That would be a grease pencil nightmare!)

Hold a cooking contest for the main course, desserts, etc., to be judged by those attending. (The only trouble here is everyone'd have to bring there items from home, cause where is all the stoves going to come from to cook them their? Then too, can you just imagine the uproar over "prejudise judging" and the like?)

You probably want to steer clear of this one.

Have a dutch-oven cook-off. (If your going to do this, be sure and get a burn permit. Ask me how I know, what with Carvell and the run-in he had with the fire department three years ago. Then there was that other time when the firemen paid us a visit, when Varland cooked up his "greenwood smoked duck." Too bad we never got to taste any but what was watered down (get it) after the firehose tipped it over pre-machurly.)

Catered Dinners:

Comparison Shop (there's that place again!). Take notes, deal with issues such as deposits and cancellation policies, talk with two references, check on convenience of location, parking, accessibility, highchairs and boosters, decorations, etc. before making deposit. This is all nice and fine, but the Farleys has never had a catered dinner in their life (that anyone can remember), unless you consider it catered that time when Moroni's roomate cooked that whatever-it-was ghoulash stuff from his home country of whatever-the-heck-place-it-was last time.

Not only did we wind up paying him a fee (when we didn't know we was going to) but almost nobody ate more than one teensy spoonfull of it once it was tasted and that was more than most anybody in the family could stomach. Plus Verlene, who was in nursing school at the time, was run ragged trying to take care of everybody but got special credit for a report she done on it which, luckily, did not make it to the newspapers). Thank goodness for the Pepto Dismol. So stand warned on this one. TRY IT OUT FIRST!

💰 Catered dinners is expensive also. It costs extra money besides because of the forced "gratuity" (now there's a Oximormon if I ever heard one!). I know, for one, the Farleys will never ever do that again as the memories is still fresh in our minds and other places.

☎ But If the ladies in your family are all cooking haters or feminests or something just make sure you phone 6-12 months in advance, then two months, then one month and parctically every day after that. And I could tell a good story about that too, but I won't. (This is good advice for every single solitary thing that goes on at the family reunion, by the way. Take this as a general rule: call everybody, more often than you would otherwise. If it doesn't work then, then it wasn't meant to.)

🍴 Offer several choices, decided ahead of time, or offer only one main choice but provide a well-stocked soup and salad bar. (If you can understand this, then good.)

👄 Have a buffet-style rather than a sit-down dinner to save on the cost of servers. (Us Farleys never hired a server in all our life. And we also tips at resteraunts for SERVICE and not because the waitress finally brings our stuff out of obligation.)

Planning for large numbers

This is really good and interesting to boot for not only your reunion but for other groups of persons and get togethers as well. Of course, it ain't Aunt Pearl's and Arvilla's formulas, for sure, but then, not everybody has boughten this book yet, either. So here goes:

🐮 Multiply out the amounts of foods shown below (only if you want to eat them, of coarse) by the number of people that you've got to feed, and they say you'll come out just about right:

Meats:	Vegetables:
1/4 lb. hamburger	1 potato
2 pieces chicken	1/2 carrot
1/2 lb. turkey	1/4 onion
1/4 lb. roast beef, pork, or	Bread:
lamb	2 rolls or biscuits
	2 slices of other bread

(The only trouble here is this don't take into account the half portions and double portions and desserts and snacks, you notice. That being the case it will certainly result in waste, expense, or maybe mad and hungry people or both! Remember the starving children in India is what I always say. You see how good Aunt Pearl is treating you?)

For some of our Top Bestest Most Popular Farley Family Recipes turn yourself over to page ~~76~~ ~~80~~ 81 👉

Leroy nearly drank gramps teeth that was in cherry seven up in the refrigerator.

Entertainment and Entertainment Budget

This here is where our currant president (my big brother) Heber J. Farley steps in on our family reunion. He is the one as runs the program every year and, believe you me, we've had some doozies. So this next is notes on entertainment as he's seen fit to do it over many years. These notes include a budget section which you can jump over to and fill out if you like. But be sure to overlook this that Heber knows about programs as it can really make or break your reunion with amazing fastness!

Notes about the Entertainment
By Heber J. Farley,
President of the Farley Family
Corporation Organization Association.

IN GENERAL:

- MOST IMPORTANT: Write everything down somewhere you can find it. This includes names and phones of people you decided you wouldn't have to have on your program in case of emergency (which is often). Carry this list with you in a very close place at all times.

- Keep a list of what everybody did at last year's reunion (and ~~hte the~~ the year before as well) and what anybody is going to do this year so that nobody does something somebody else could have done instead.

- Keep it simple as you can and inexpensive. People don't come to a reunion for entertainment but for family porposes.

- Always use of the talents of family members if at all pOssible.

> #1 it is cheap
> #2 It makes people come
> #3 It is usually really funny if its not good (but sometimes it is)
> #4 It helps build family talents
> #5 It gives the children something to do besides tare things down

- Perfessional entertainers are expensive but a real option for variebility. (Make sure you see them first if you hire, though. You could wind up paying either way!)

- Prepare for hte unknown. Something unknown happens everytime since I been president, and if you're ready for it then everybody will be happier. And coupled to this

- Don't panic. Everybody looks to you to be in charge and run things nicely. If you go up in a cloud of smoke where does that leave everybody at hte fire?

MUSIC:

People have gotten used to music everyhwhere from hte mall including the dentists chair. This kind of thing should definately be included.

- Prerecorded or live music during registration to set about hte reinforcemant of your family theme.

- Music from a particular culture or era is good

- Hired musicians is expensive even if they're real nice including—pianoist, strolling guitarist, string quartet, DJ, singer, harpest or hte etc.

- Always make room for singing family songs. (run copies off in advance) This is fun for everybody and results in more family harmOny.

- Good to remember: there is usually somebody in every family that is good in electronix. If you can get him to do it, it will usually be free from charge (the sound, microphone and etc. .)

THE ACTUAL PROGRAM ITSELF, (formal or informal or otherwise):(you will want to include many of hte following AS YOU CAN but don't feel you have to include all of them, you will see what I mean:) *(P.S. Their are always other choices but you have to usually push them.)*

- Its better to start with a opening sOng. This could be your family song (if you don't have one, get one!).

- ~~The~~ the acknowledgements to committee members, hard workers, or s(ecial guests. Some jokes about them (that aren't mean) would be good here.

- reports to the family on business of the family

- announcements or reminders for other reunion activities or future reunion plans

67

- performances from talented family members, such as clogging, baton twirling, poetry reading, skits, singing, playing instruments and things and etc. or

- you could have a real live talent show (with prizes for winners) *(P.S. Danger! This can get real ugly, being as since everybody thinks there kid is the winner!)*

- a brief toasting to hte family (if they got glasses or pop) (One family I know actually awards prizes for the best toast so they toast for about a half hour, but it runs up their food bill some.)

- you can give clever or funny awards (like for the last one to arrive or hte one with hte most kids at hte reunion. This is good for those as doesn't get recognition awards too often.)

- give away of door prizes. These can be anything from Arvillas Black Forest cake to family genealogy sheets. Don't go overboard on buying things though, because who will pay?

- family spe3ches. About hte family (but keep them short or comical or both– this is hard to do).

- hold an "in memorandum" service, prayer, or moment of silence for ancestors or for those who have passed away since hte last reunion

- the reciting of ~~hte~~ the family motto like "Everythings better when we do it together" or "Thank the Lord we made it here again this year," or "It takes one to know one."

- and finally, hire performers only if there no other choices *(P.S. Ther's allways other choices.)*

- Oh and this last here. There is sure to be sOme person needs to speak who isn't going to ask you and who wouldn't normally get asked to s(eak. But just who this person is or why they need to speak hte Lord alone knows, so I suggest that you hunt down this special person (man or woman) before each program. It is always gratifying to all who are gathered to hear their words.

OTHER TYPE ACTIVITIES:

- a family bulletin board (or tree or chalkboard or one family used their old car) on which to post family news like babies born, missions, marriages, military, family trips, awards, scholarships, photos, where to meet and hte like.

- family association meeting (for adults)

- Stearing committe meeting (for hte stearing comittee)

- quilt making (for raffle or auction or a new baby) It takes yOu half hte time when you're working with professionals like Aunt Pearl.

- field trips to local spots of interest

- games that involve many people and a lot of interaction

- dancing

- fashion show- sports for large numbers, such as volleyball, soccer or softball

- old-fashioned games, such as sack races, three-legged races, wheelbarrow races, egg or water balloon toss, bobbing for apples, tug-of-war, horseshoes

- campfire singing or story-telling

- If your reunion is not in a rural setting have a weenie or marshmellow rOast around a hubatchi cooker set up in the middle of the cement.

PEARL'S OF WISDOM
A burn in the
hand is worth two
in the brush

- a game where you guess who this is, using pictures of older family members when they was little.

- have a real nice photogra(h made of hte whole family. This is hard to get them all together and no one thinks they look like themselves but everybody else does.

(P.S. You need to get a real photographer who knows how to take actual pictures. If you have someone in the family do it and it flops everybody will be mad at the one who took it. Us Farleys have always found it best to get a real photographer and let the family members each buy there own pictures.)

IDEAS FOR THE KIDS (Your for sure going to want to put somebody else in charge on this):

- group activities, such as hayrides, sports, relay races, hiking, kids-only parties, swimming, skating, games, contests

- adult activities with a fun slant (family history, crafts, skits performed as part of the prOgram, talent show to present to adults, old movies, slides, memory books, picture books).

- cartoons on ~~hte~~ ~~the~~ the video

- a fish pond (where you put up a sheet) and dangle the pole over to catch some little prize or snack.

DECORATIONS (nice but not necessarily necessary):
- flower arrangements, flags, banners, balloons
- items like shirts or hats with family logo, crest, motto or things upOn it
- place settings, table cloths   *(p.s. this is not food)*
- helium balloon centerpieces (4-7 latex balloons with 1 mylar in hte middle)

- dessert cakes centerpieces (as give aways)
- napkins and coasters with crest or logo
- and there's just whole lots more. The trick is to use your inner creative juices to make things work for your own particular family. And that's all I got to say.

Heber J. Farley

Heber, good on ya! My goodness, but that older brother of mine knows his stuff, don't he? When you get your information from those as has gone on before, there is certainly something to be learned from each and every person, exspecially those as was in charge and knows what it is their talking about.

However, you may have noticed Heber never got around to getting down to the budget. If I interpret right, I think what he was trying to say, if I can read it right, that it totally depends upon what you do. If your family only likes sports then the major thing is to get a field or something. And if they like to do shows, then you better get a place you can do shows, and if your all campers then thats what you got to find places for. BUT (another big BUT), keeping it all in the family is a whole lot cheaper way than any other way.

Entertainment Budget

To Figure your entertainment budget, note down these costs (which should all come from the committee chairman as they should know if anybody does):

rentals on places, field, campgrounds, & etc.	$_____
rentals for equipment (volleyball nets or snowmobiles, or microphones etc.)	$_____
to buy prizes, awards, decorations, shirts, and stuff	$_____
rental on movies and games for kids	$_____
any cost for perfessional entertainment the family hired	$_____
the shooting cost of the photographer	$_____
all other missellaneous costs	$_____
Add these all up for the Total Entertainment Budget	$_____

Boy, I hope you was sitting down. I forgot to warn you.

You may have wanted to because the entertainment budget is always way higher than anybody else expected. Its a lot like taxes.

Phew!

Okay, good work! That's a heap of info, on budgets, ain't it? (And look how fast you done it, too!)

Now that you got together your most hardest totals, this is the junction where you ought to clap for yourself as nobody else is going to! What we've got next here next is the **Actual Total Reunion Budget Planner Worksheet**. I would like to advise you to Xerox this worksheet page plenty instead of actually using it, because you'll be erasing it, scribbling in the edges, tearing, or wadding it up and tossing it a whole lot more than you think without thinking. This being the case, I would suggest you make about ten or more of these at first (more if you want to show them to your Comittees or Family Heads).

//// STOP! BIG HUGE WARNING! ////

Now as you done all this work your feeling pretty good and I don't blame you. BUT, you got to remember everybody doesn't think as clear as you do now. Remember in a strong way the law of COMMON CONSENT. These budgets you worked so dang hard on can go right up in smoke in the chimley unless you remember this one thing:

> **PEARL'S OF WISDOM**
> People only pay
> for what they want, and
> they got to want it bad if
> YOU are buying it with
> THERE money.

Entertainment Budget

What this means is that the family reunion should only provide the things that everybody truly agrees to pay for all T-O-G-E-T-H-E-R . . . And that is UP FRONT! (which most times is a heckuva decision all by itself—but I leave that up to you and your own personal close family to fix). I cannot say this strong enough. WATCH OUT!! Some others will want a catered this or a "cook your own" that. It just depends totally on what kind of family you got. Maybe you don't even know what you got yet . . . pay attention. Its important. Trust me! I'm telling you true.

Anyhow, okay, here is the FAMILY REUNION BUDGET WORK SHEET I told you about wear you can write down all your numbers and add up what its going to cost your family for there get together. Do this now and prepare for a pretty stiff lemonaid and a rest afterwards.

FAMILY REUNION BUDGET WORK SHEET

Budget Item	Budget Costs
Travel subsidee (including subsidee if any)	$_____
Entertainment (if any)	$_____
Pool charges	$_____
Photography	$_____
Food	$_____
Lodging (including subsidee if any)	$_____
Mailings	$_____
Telephonings	$_____
Printing	$_____
Decorations	$_____
Extra diapers, personal effects, cleaning stuff etc.	$_____
Rentals (video, games, skis, bolleyballs, etc.)	$_____
Family dues (the yearly type)	$_____
Campground or other reservational fees	$_____
Mail back (for lost items)	$_____
TOTAL REUNION BUDGET	$_____

Derive Ten % of this total Number (x .1 =_____) And add it on (As a contingentsy and for saftey). You will be perfectly amazed how much this saves your cookies and makes you sleep at night.

THE TOTAL REUNION TOTAL BUDGET PLUS CONTINGENTSY:$_____

Whew! Scarey ain't it?! Once you got all the numbers added up you have reached your TOTAL REUNION TOTAL BUDGET PLUS CONTINGENTSY total then here is exactly what you do:

Take this number that comes up at the GRAND TOTAL sign (above)

And DIVIDE by the total number of persons (big and little) attending (or saying they'll attend as we've talked about)   ÷_____

Equals the magic dreadful terrifying actual per person cost to put on the reunion (read it and weep). $_____

75

This here is the whole ball of wax! You can't get there by any other way but what we already done! And two bits to ten that it'll change as soon as it is known as to what it is! No such thing as over planning!

With this number under your belt now everybody has to be let know. Most exspecially the ACTUAL PAYERS. WHAT IS A ACTUAL PAYER? A Actual Payer might could be a father, a step-mother, a boyfriend, a cousin, a gramma, an aunt, or in other words the responsible parties over the unresponsible parties. The ACTUAL PAYERS doesn't even have to show up to the family reunion, but they **got to** auntie up so's the reunion can actually take place. This here is the amount you absolutely got to accumulate from each and every one of the ACTUAL PAYERS through to the time till the reunion.

PEARL'S OF WISDOM
Don't be caught holding the bag with no money in it.

Now some can do it in one big chunk or they can make even two or three monthly payments (which is a kind of headache all its own but some families does it that way). Others again has a monthly kitty which grows (and gets interest down to the bank) until such time as it is needed. But the treasurer has to be clear and smart about the bookkeeping. (You'd sure hate to arrive and be accused of mooching when you paid anyhow.)

Okay here's a couple of last shots on this budget business:

• When called upon to do so, announce costs loud and clear so as to avoid any misunderstandings.

• Set up a refund policy (this is most exspecially important to be done before the fact and not after, as I know for a fact that there is some people will ask for a full or partial refund every single year for some teensy little reason, and if you don't have guidelines on that stuff, well, everybody is going to be unhappy, because one refund changes everything!).

That's why I always figure in a 10% contingentsy for everything, that way with bring ins, extras, and refunds your not caught with your nikkers down.

• Don't spend everything right down to the nubbins. Leave some in the account for seed money next year.

• Opennness and frankness about money matters is just so important. If you can't explain when and why and such - then your in deep ketchup!

- and -

• And last the best of all the game:

PEARL'S OF WISDOM
Have a vote weigh
before the fact on nearly
everything, that way it
ain't your fault

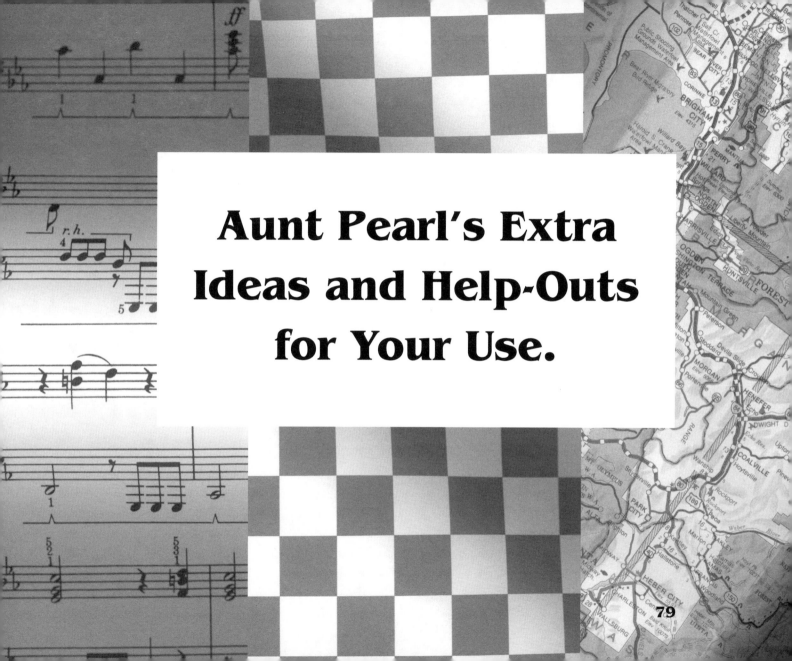

Aunt Pearl's Extra Ideas and Help-Outs for Your Use.

Right to left:
5. Marva,
4. Viola,
3. Pearl ...Me
2. Beatrice
1. Arvilla

The time each one of us brought exactly the same Jello salad. a example of Farley Telegraphy (so says Beatrice)

"For More than 50" RECIPES

The Farley Family Bestest and
Most Biggest Recipes—(no foolin'!)

BRACED SHORT RIBS

24 to 26 lbs beef short ribs
1 c. flour
1 c. lard or drippings
6 tbsp salt
1 tsp pepper
1 1/2 grated onion
3 c meat stock or water
2 qt. chopped carrots
4 qt. chopped green peppers
2 qt. chopped celery

Drag meat in flour. Brown slowly on all sides in lard or drippings; season. Add onions and meat stock (or water). Cover tightly. Cook in 300 degree oven or simmer on top of range for 1 hour and 30 minutes to 2 hours or until tender. Add vegetables, cook about 15 minutes. Remove meat; thicken liquid enough to make gravy. Serve vegetables, gravy and short ribs together.

Yeild: approx. 50 servings.

LOOKOUT CHILI

25 lbs chili meat
5 lbs onions, finely chopped
1/4 lb garlic, finely chopped
8 small cans tomato paste
1/4 cup cumin powder
1 1/2 lbs chili powder or to taste
1 1/2 lbs lard
6 to 8 qt. boiling water
4 c flour

Sear meat a small amount at a time. Mix in onions and garlic. Add tomato paste, seasonings, lard, and water; stir occasionally. Cook slowly for 3 hours. Parch flour; add to chili just before serving.

Yield: approx. 65 servings.

CHOOSER'S CHILIBURGER FILLING

20 lbs minced beef
Fat
2 c flour
5 tbsp curry powder
4 tsp bay leaf
1/2 bottle of Worcestershire sauce
5 bottles tomato catsup
10 raw potatoes, finely grated

Brown meat in small amount of fat; add onions and flour. When mixture is well browned, add remaining ingredients. Simmer until potatoes are well done; mash potaoes into the meat. Serve hot in hamburger buns, if desired.

Yeild: approx. 100 servings.

SUPER SLOPPY JOES

20 lbs hamburger
1 1/2 gal catsup
1/2 c dry mustard
3/4 c lemon juice
2 c brown sugar
4 qt sliced celery (optional)
1 pt ground onions
Pineapple juice (optional)

Brown beef; drain off excess fat. Combine catsup, mustard, lemon juice, brown sugar. Add celery, onions, and a small amount of pineapple juice. Add to meat. Simmer until of desired doneness.

Yeild: Approx.100 Servings

"HELLO" HAMBURGER LOAF

6 lbs hamburger
3 lbs pork sausage
6 eggs, beaten
Salt and pepper to taste
1 box soda crackers crumbled
1 stalk celery, finely chopped
6 carrots grated
4 onions, finely chopped
1 pt. tomato juice
1 bottle catsup

Mix hamburger with sausage. Combine eggs, seasonings, and cracker crumbs. Add celery, carrots, and onions. Add to meats, mix thoroughly. Add tomato juice and catsup. Shape into loaf. Place in loaf or dripper pan. Place pan in pan of water, cover with foil. Bake at 375 degrees for 3-4 hours.

Yield: approx. 35-40 servings.

GIMME SA MORE!

2 c. chopped onions
4 tbsp butter
8 lbs ground meat
3 c chopped green peppers
12 8oz cans tomato sauce
2 can whole kernal corn
4 tbsp chili pepper
Salt to taste
2 lb medium noodles, cooked
2 lb grated cheddar cheese

Saute onions in butter in skillet; add meat. Cook until brown. Add all remaining ingredients except cheese and noodles: mix well. Combine mixture with noodles. Turn into 6-quart casserole; top with cheese. Bake until mixture is bubbly and cheese melted.

Yield: approx. 50-60 servings

DIFFERNT SLOPPY JOE MIX

12 lbs ground beef
4 c chopped onions
2 c fat or suet
1 cup flour
2/3 c salt
2 tsp pepper
1 c chili powder
4 tsp paprika
4 tsp sugar
4 tsp monosodium glutamate
4 tsp tabasco sauce
2 1/2 qt tomatoe sauce
6 qt kidney beans
6 c water

Brown ground beef and onions in fat; add flour and seasonings. Cook for 10 minutes. Add tomato sauce, beans, and water. Cook slowly for 1 hour and 30 minutes or until thick. Serve hot on buns.

Yeild: 100 servings

HOBO (suicide) STEW

18 lbs hamburger or stew meat
15 qt water
5 tbsp salt
1 tbsp monosodium glutamate
1 1/2 tsp. Pepper
1 tbsp thyme
3/4 cup parsley
6 bay leaves
6 beef bullion cubes
18 large carrots, diced
30 large potatoes, diced
72 green onions, diced
6 pkg frozen peas, diced

Fry meat in large kettle. Add water, seasonings, buillon cubes, carrots, and potatoes. Add onions and peas, cook over low heat until vegetables are tender.

Yield: 50 servings

BAKED HAM IN YOUR BLANKET

1 24-30 lbs ham
8 c flour
2 c brown sugar
4 tbsp ground cloves
4 tbsp ground cinnamon
4 tbsp mustard
2 tsp pepper
3 c water, cider, or vinegar

Trim off end, rind, and greater part of fat from ham. Place in open roasting pan, fat side up. Mix flour with remaining ingredients into dough. Make dough into sheet large enough to cover ham. Place in cold oven; turn heat to 300 degress and bake till done.

Yield: 50-60 servings

IDAHO HAM LOAF

12 lbs ground ham
12 lbs ground lean pork
14 cups dry bread crumbs
24 eggs beaten
14 cups milk
4 tsp gound pepper

Combine all ingredients; mold into loaves in bread pans. Bake at 350 degrees for 1 hour.

Yield: 70-80 servings

MOCKING CHICKEN

6 lbs sausage
6 large onions chopped
3 green peppers, chopped
3 bunch celery chopped
27 cups boiling water
9 pkg chicken noodle soup mix
7 1/2 cups uncooked rice
1 1/2 lbs almonds

Brown sausage. Add onions, green peppers, and celery. Cook for 10 minutes. Pour boiling water over soup mix; add rice. Stir in sausage mixture and almonds, reserving some almonds for top. Place in two casseroles or one large pan. Bake at 350 degrees for 1 hour or until done. Sprinkle with remaining almonds.

Yield: 60 servings

PINEAPPLE-PRUNE-UPSIDE-DOWN LOAF

6 c brown sugar
1 1/2 c melted butter
60 slices pinapple
16 lbs ground ham
8 c soft bread crumbs
16 eggs
8 oz prepared mustard
2 c brown sugar
2 tsp pepper
60 stewed prunes

Mix brown sugar with butter. Pour into pan. Arrange pineapple slices in rows in pan. Mix ham with remaining ingredients except prunes. Pat on top of pineapple. Bake at 350 degrees for 35-40 minutes. Cut into squares with one pineapple slice per serving. Top each square with a prune.

Yield: 60 servings

GROUNDED ITALIAN SANDWICHES

35 lbs ground bologna
1/2 gal relish
2 gal salad dressing
1 can evaporated milk
6 dozen hard-cooked eggs,
    chopped or ground.
1 18 oz jar of mustard
50 (1 lb 8 oz) loaves sandwich
    bread

Divide meat and remaining ingredients in two 25 qt dish pans. Mix well. Season with salt and pepper to taste. Spread on sandwich bread.

Yield: 600 servings unless you pile it on thick

OPENING SOCIAL SALAD

30 lbs chicken breasts
9 large bunches of celery, diced
    diaganolly
9 no. 2 cans of minted pineapple
    chunks
3 lbs broken pecans
3 qt salad dressing
90 lettuce cups

Simmer chicken breasts in a small amount of salted water until tender. Refrigerate until cool; dice and refrigerate immediately until ready to mix. Just before serving, mix all ingredients except lettuce. Serve on lettuce cups.

Yeild: approx. 90 servings

PEARLENE'S PASTIES

4 1/2 lbs shortening
14 lbs flour
Salt
Ice water
15 lbs round steak trimmed and
    boned
Pepper
22 lbs potatoes, peeled and cut
    into 1/2 in. cubes
4 lbs Onions, peeled and shredded
1 lb margarine or butter.

Cut shortening into flour and 6 table-spoonfuls of salt. Add enough ice water to make a firm dough. Roll dough 1/8 in. thick. Cut into 9 in. circles. Cut beef into 1/2 in. cubes. Mix suet with beef; add salt and pepper to taste. Mix potatoes with onions and salt to taste. Place 1 cup potato mixture and 1/2 cup meat in center of each circle of dough. Dot generously with margarine. Moisten edges with water. Bring top and bottom portions of dough together; pinch edges together securely. Fold slightly; flute edges. Place on greased cookie sheet without touching. Bake at 375 degrees for 1 hour. Serve with catsup and additional butter.

Yeild: 50 servings

89

10 Bestest Farley Spots for Family Reunions

Now I'm sure this title could possibily mislead you into thinking I'm going to give a way our top secret places for family reunions...well, that'll come later. First though, you got to realize that everybody's not going to be happy anyplace, and somebody's going to hate everyplace, and somebody's not, so you got to find somebody who can be happy and it might just as well be you!

And as to the place, I can definately say just like all them realters says, its location, Its Location, ITS LOCATION! Since are people in the North don't want to go all the way South and the Dixieites don't like coming all the way North, we learned to sort of meet in the middle. Outside our own family houses (where its cheap), here is the top best middles we have found.

#10. Sand Dunes

Now there's alots of different ones in Utah (Arvilla says dig down about 3 and 1/4 inches anywhere in Utah and you got sand). Anyways, our little kids who likes sandpiles sure gets a kick out of it and them older kids whose got them sand jitneys do too. But remember, your bringing home enough sand in your hair to set your rug cleaning back a year, as well as clog your pipes, the food is full of it (no matter how you pack it), and even Norda, who is a real outdoorsy-type, says sleeping on sand is just this side of cement, so think before you sleep. (I was in the camper.)

DIRECTIONS: go down I-15 till you get to the Santequin exit and go off till it turns south about Eureka and go and go until you get to Jericho Junktion where you see sign saying, Little Sahara Recreation Area. That's your first clue, and where you head off to the right — West. (If your coming from the south you can go straight over from Nephi (which is another way you can come from the North or turn off for Delta and go up through Lynndyl.) There's also supposed to be some sand up by Eureka and other places, but I never seen them yet.

#9. Yuba Lake

Now there didn't used to be a fee here and things but its still a nice little lake and lots of nice camp grounds and room to wander. Its got nice

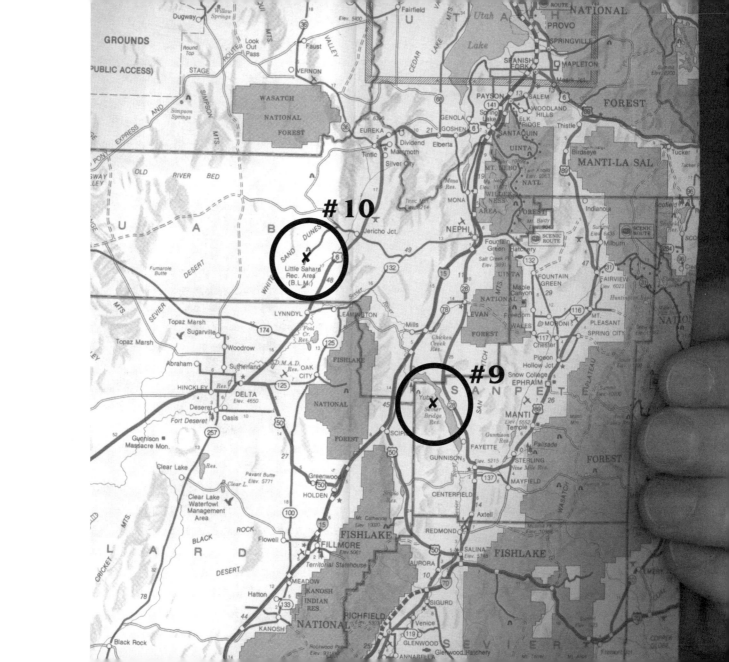

beaches on the north (where they won't let you camp anymore, go figure), and they got cliffs to dive from, but be careful on this as Uncle Vaughan has never quite been the same since he smacked his head one time. Still its one of the Farleys favorites. Problem is nearly every scout troop between thither and yon is up there in July, so bare that in mind. We rented them water machines and all the people who could ride them had a good time. The rest of us watched. Oh, and Leroy fell out of the boat and wet hisself prettygood!

DIRECTIONS: Go down or up I-15 till you see the signs and go there. Its kind of past Nephi and before Scipio or vicy versey. You can't see it till you come over the hill.

#8. Silver Lake

Okay, its another pretty nice little lake away up there and its real high up but not as much as it used to be when nobody knew it was up there. And there's lots of places around there to camp and explore. Still its cold at night all year round which hurt my bronkitus quite considerable that year. Moroni lost the twins for about five and a half hours which was the quietest things ever was. (He found them in somebody else's tent asleep.)

DIRECTIONS: Go on up American Fork Canyon and take the left tong (not the loop) and just keep going straight up till you get there.

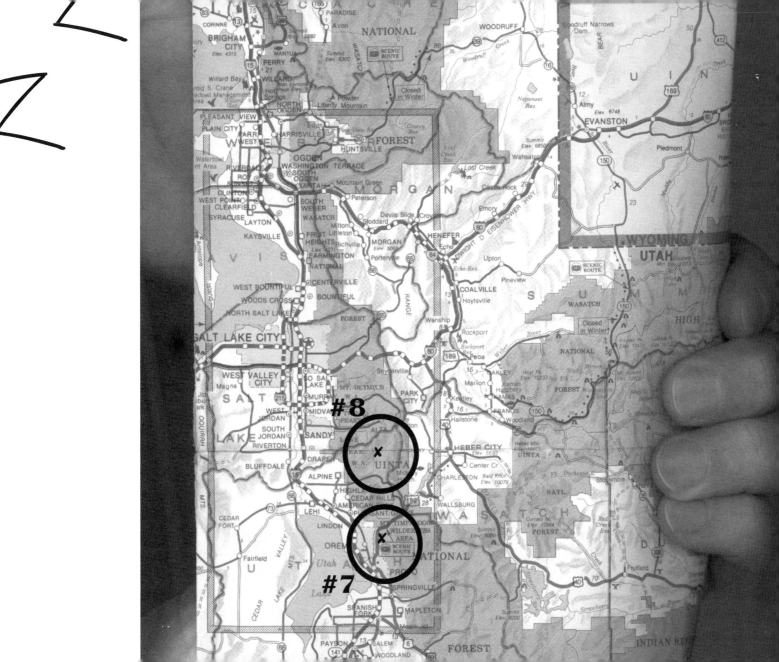

#7. Bridle Vaile Falls

There is alots of camping all up and down the Provo Canyon. And the little cable car runs clean to the top of the mountain nearly and you can feel like your in Europe in Switzerland. Ooo la la, unless, of coarse, your hight-sick like Ferrell who urped up all over the car on the way up. (We made him shut his eyes on the way down.) Also there is nice side-trips up to Sundance (Once I thought I seen Robert Redford in a red sports car with sunglasses on. But he was going the other direction.) Cascade Springs is nice but you can't camp there no more. Deer Creek reseuvoire is right up there, too and you can always drop down to Provo for groceries or a movie and stuff.

DIRECTIONS: Just go up or down Provo Canyon till you see it.

#6. Dutch John

Hardly don't nobody ever think of going East unless the relatives out there make a fuss about it. (Usually they like coming in is the truth of it) but anyhows this is on the Flaming Gourge reseuvoire out by Vernal. Its quite nice with alots of things to do like the Dinosaur Quorry, the Utah Fieldhouse of Natural History and Dinosaur Gardens, and the Ladies of the Whitehouse Doll Collection at the library (I done all these

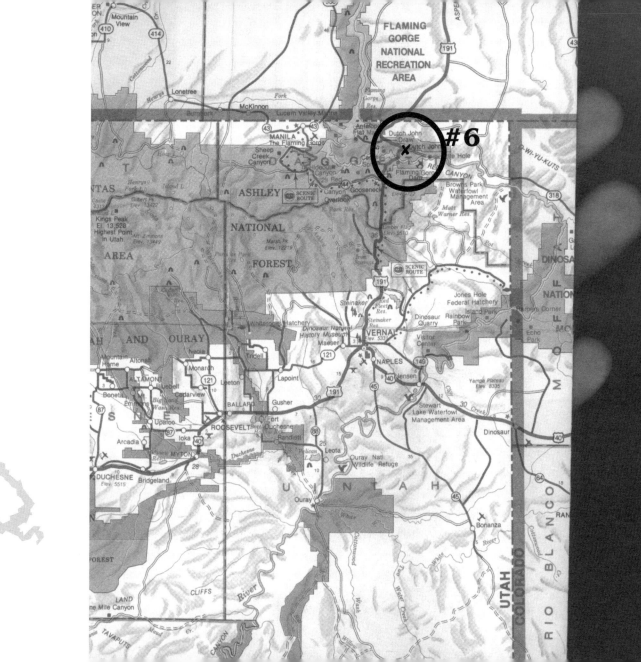

#6

whilst everybody else was playing in the water.) Oh, and theirs Indian petrogliffs on the cliffs there which is really amazing considering how they done it. Skipper, Bud, and Cleetus made some in chalk that I didn't think was half so good (and neither did the forest ranger who took them away). And Dripping Springs. Well, like I says, you'll never want for something to see.

DIRECTIONS: Come onto Vernal on Highway 40 when you get to Halfway Hollow your 3/4 there. At Vernal go up North on 191 till you run into Flaming Gourge and lots of markers tell you to see the dinosaur age your in. Dutch John is 3 miles North East (up right) on FS#75. We camped on the left.

#5. Anybodies Cabin

This is not actually the name of a cabin but means anybodies cabin you can barrow or (gulp) rent. (Bye the way, Cabin is just the name for a house built in the woods, so don't be on the lookout for Davey Crockets house or Abraham Linclon). Now this is a okay idea unless that it rains hard like it done in '92 when we had over sixty people sleeping in a cabin that was there for maybe 12. When Heber got up three times in the night to go to the bathroom it woke up apromixmately 20 people each time and everybody was real crabby for three days, not to mention cramped. And there was mesquitoes after. And once it snowed in June when we was all in shirtsleeves, so let that serve as a lesson.

DIRECTIONS: Name of the canyon and then paper plates with your name on it till you get there.

#4. Sandy Beach

Now I know nobodies heard of this place and thats good. It makes it more remoat. See, its down to the South part of Utah Lake where there is a beach there, but only sometimes, depending on how high or low the-water is (which also changes from June to September.) Its real windy nearly always and you can fly kites and its really shallow for them kids to wade in and its warm (expecially compared with some of these moun-tains lakes that is like the Titantic Iceburg). Here again, though, you got sand, but not nearly so much. Venida lost all her silverware set in the sand there when the kids buried it for fun and then couldn't remember where, so if you find it let us know.

DIRECTIONS: Get off at the second Springville exit (unless your coming from the south and then its the first) and go away from Springville to the West for a ways till the road starts to bend back South. After that take your first road right till you come to Sweden road (its dirt, but don't worry). If you crossed the bridge you went too far. Go down

Sweden along the river till you get to the lake. If there's sand there, you found it. If there's not, the waters too high and sorry about that.

#3. Keetly

One of the in-laws had some land up there and it is so pretty and nice, just like you imagine a little Swedish fyord or valley or something with a nice little river to boot. It makes you wonder why people don't come there more often. Its like being in a little piece of heaven (with volleyball). The mountain air does a body good and there's hardly nobody there and easy to get to. Its also a good jump off for the Uinta's (where some went to spend the night.) Of coarse, the Memmott's (with all their money) spent most of their time in Park City (which is right close) going to the silver mine, eating out, and looking for Art. I never did find out who he was but he seems like a big deal in Park City as I heard a lots about him too. This was one of our best years. Of course we was up when everybody else was out, seems like.

DIRECTIONS: You can go up from Salt Lake by I-80 and get off at highway forty (the second Park City exit) and head for Heber and its just down there about 18 miles. (If you've went to Hailstone, you're too far.) If you've got to come from Provo you head up to Heber and keep going left passed Hailstone to Keetly.

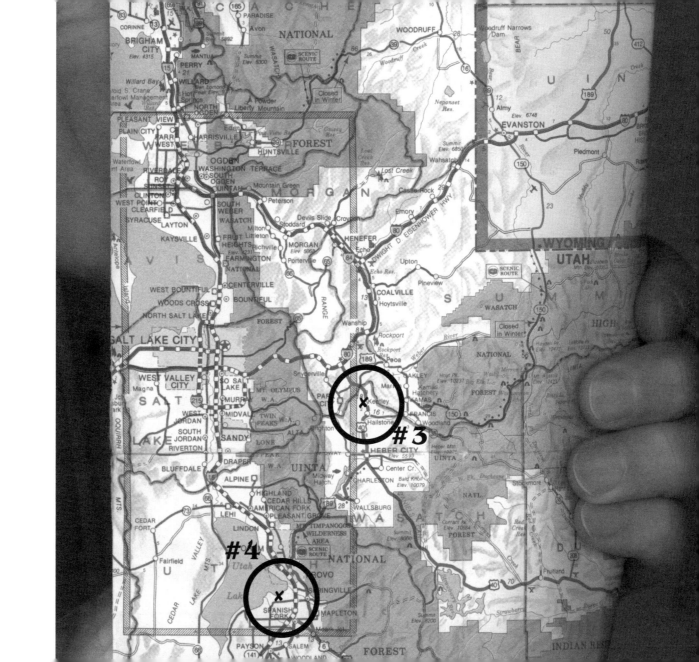

#2. Delta

I know its a little more South but most of these has been Northy. This area is so neat because of there is so many interesting things right close by and don't cost nothing. There is smaller sand dunes (as almost nobody knows about) there is a little volcano, there is superhot springs, there is caves, there is real topazes that you can dig out for yourself, and also black sand to pan gold with, and a old fort, and Clear Lake nearby to boot! Verlo has always said there ought to be a place like Disneyland downthere and its a good idea but he doesn't have enough money. Sometimes a little hot summers but worth it, that is, if you know what your looking for.

DIRECTIONS: Same as the Sand Dunes only don't turn off.

And the #1 bestest place we ever had our reunion to:

#1. The Rest Stop

Just before you comeout of the mountains above Cove Fort (which is past fillmore about 60 miles)or up top if your going North past Cove Fort from the South) there is this neat little Rest Stop tucked away up on the side of the mountain. Grampa got marooned there one year in his car. They called us, and so the whole family just picked up and went down there. We pitched our tents and campers, had games, plenty of

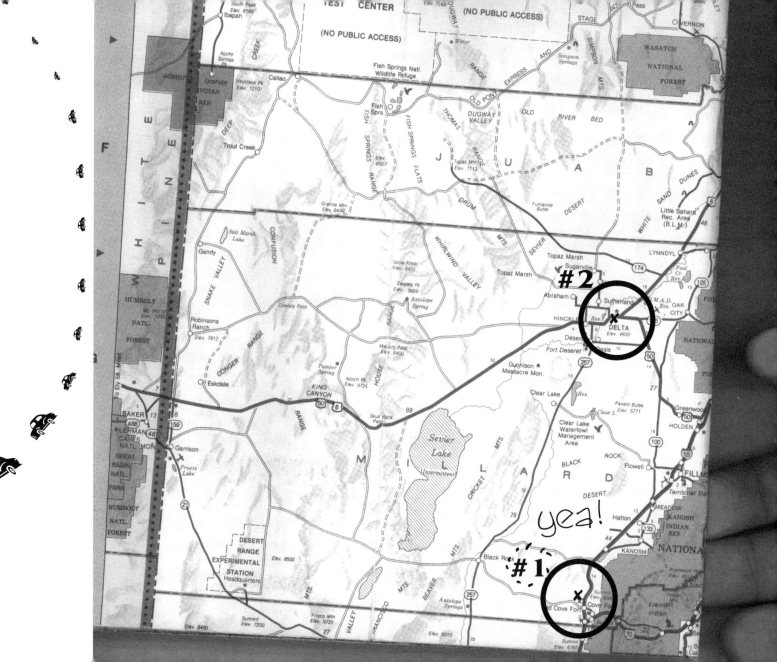

bathrooms, and lots of fun until the Highway Patrol come. But even at that, once he'd had a hotdog and some of Twilla's cinnamin twists he didn't even kick us off till after night and we was all done then anyways. It was the best place we ever had. And lots of nice people passing through. And one of the bestest things about it was that we sold all our leftovers to passersbys and made a prophet that year! Wilford used to take a nap there whenever we went South or North everytime after that.

"Uncle Earl" the man who passed hisself off as an uncle just to eat.

PRESTON EDWARD MEMMOT II, PH.D.

A Sparse but Useful Glossary and Pronunciation Guide of Native Idioms

By Preston Edward Memmot II, Ph.D.

To: Anyone in or out of the Farley family who may or may not be attending the annual family reunion in or out of Utah.

Re: The linguistics of the Farleys (the environs of Utah).

Though the Farleys have many lovable, admirable, and even uplifting qualities, these can be overshadowed by their parochial accent (which they think is nonexistent.) This accent, along with severe regionalisms, is sometimes difficult for visitors or people outside the family and/or Utah culture to decipher. With that in mind I offer this simple, though noncomprehensive, lesson in what I and others have come to call "Utahnics" (pronounced yew-TAH-neeks) or sometimes known as "'Merican Farkism."

Utahnics is apparently a genetically based form of communication among natives of Utah, southern Idaho, and parts of Arizona and Nevada. It is apparently descended from the pioneers of Brigham Young's old territory of Deseret. Whether Brigham himself spoke in this unusual fashion is a tantalizing but, as yet, unresolved mystery.

Because of recent moves to authenticate subcultural ethnic languages and/or speech patterns, Utah School Districts are considering recognizing Utahnics as a separate language and securing federal funds to preserve it. This is demonstrated by the fact that some of this report has been taken from the internet. For any traveler into the state, here are a few representative terms and a little overview retrieved from my personal Utahnics thesaurus:

"Air" - our
"Expecially" - especially
"Librel" - liberal
"Irregardless" - anyways
"Simular" - similar
"Tore" (as "In Paris, we took the sight-seeing tore.")
"Spacial" - special
"Reelize" - realize
"Franteek" - frantic
"Patriartical" - patriarchal or patriotic
"Grajulee" - gradually
"Groz(h)" - garage

"Favert" - favorite
"Bleev" - believe
"Probly" - probably
"Spart" - spirit
"Exposta" - supposed to
"anyhows" - anyway
"lyberry" - library
"Youbetcha" - yes

Dropping syllables is a direct outgrowth of the inherent spartan nature or "thriftiness" of most Utahns. Some shortened sentences have been aped by other areas of the United States but actually began in Utah where state communication is best if short.

"Djeet?"- Did you eat?
"Cha"- Are you? as in "Whatcha doing?"
"Ain'tcha?"- Aren't you?
"Dja?"- Did you?
"Djew?"- Did you? (Panguitch version)
"Squeet"- Let's go eat
"Wannoo" - Want to
"Yore" - You are
"Sco" - Let's go

Here is a typical Utahnics conversation using these foreshortened phrases (and two medium expletives):

LaVerl: "Djeet yet?"
LaVell: "Keyrud, no! Djew?"
LaVar: "Fetch! Squeet."
LaVerl: "Wannoo?"
All: "Shir! Youbetcha! Sco!"

One of the most interesting interpolations of the "Utahnics" accent is the changing of simple vowels for new ones such as "e" for "i" and vice versa:

"Ten" - tin
"Tin" - ten

107

"Git"- get
"Wint" - went
"Still" - steel
"Stell" - still
"Rill" - real
"Rilly" - really, as in "She says she rilly likes you!"
"Rully" - really, a sarcastic reply - as in reply to the above (angrily) "Rully . . ."
"Hiya" - How are you? To which most people respond, "Rully good!"
"Pello" - Pillow
"Mell" - mail, male, or mill
"Sell" - sale
"Beg" - bag, as in "A mell man carries a beg."

And these words turn the short "e" sound to a diphthong:

"playsure, maysure, traysure" - pleasure, measure, treasure

An interesting usage, which may revert to the many early English converts migrating to Utah, has resulted from the decidedly cockney use of a dropped "h" in many words such as he:

"Ee" - he: "Ee got ees mel."
"Eem" - him: "I'll go git'eem."
"Ees" - he's, his: "Ees got ees fishpole with eem."
"Dee" - did he: "Where dee go?"
"See" or "Zee" - is he: "What see doeen now?" or "Where zee live?"
"Sees" or "Zees" - is his: "What zees number?"

Another interesting cockney influence is the glottal stop in the youthful lexicon represented here by an asterisk:

"Whu* " - what, as in the infamous "Whu'ever . . ."
"Bu* " - but or butt
"Moun*un" - mountain
"Foun*un" - fountain
"Bo*ul" - bottle

"Ki*e" - kite
"Nee* " - neat
"Que* " - cute
"impor*nt" - important
"Nu*" - nut
"Kni*" - knit
"Shoo*" - shoot - an expletive
"Dangi*" - dangit - an expletive

The above long "e" sound is also used at the end of double or multiple syllabic words:

"Conservateev" - conservative
"Representateev" - representative
"Subjecteev" - subjective
"Garbeedge" - garbage
"Cabbeedge" - cabbage
"Parenteedge" - parentage
"Hemoreedge" - hemorrhage

This is closely followed by the dropping of the "g" and substituting "ee" for the "i" to any word ending in "ing."

"Shooteen" - shooting, also "runneen - hunteen - singeen - sleepeen, etc."
"Washeen" - washing, as in "The capital of our country is "Washeenton, D. C."
 (although in "Relief Society Utahnics" this can also be "Worhseen" see below)
This long "e" sound is carried to words with an -ic or -ick ending:
"Fantasteek" - fantastic
"Spasteek" - spastic
"Chroneek" - chronic

"Plasteek" - plastic
"Realisteek" - realistic
"Hydrauleek" - hydraulic
"Ethieek" - ethic
"Subjeekt" - subject -
"Atheleteek" - athletic
"Authenteek" - authentic
"Franteek" - frantic
"Sarcasteek" - sarcastic
"Mageek" - magic

Oddly enough, though unexplainable, words that actually begin with this widely used long "e" sound are underdeveloped to a short "u" sound. Some of these words are also foreshortened:

"Uhmoshnal" - emotional
"Uhmergency" - emergency
"Uhlasteek" - elastic
"Uhlongate" - elongate
"Uhleven" - eleven

Directions in Utah universally mystify travelers, but comprehension is fairly simple once you understand how streets are platted. Nearly all streets are laid either north to south or east to west on a grid that meets at the corner of main and center streets (South Temple in Salt Lake City). To find an address, it must be stated clearly in two distinct parts: 222 East (on) 4500 South (street). The first number is the house number and the first word (*north, south, east* or *west*) tells in what area the house is found. Inserting the word "on" after this first word helps you understand that the number that follows is A) the name of the street and B) the cross location of a street. This becomes more apparent with a light amount of study (which is highly recommended to any traveler who will need to drive).

But the foregoing is only to help you with written or formal addresses. The cautious traveler should be well warned that, though Utahns are extremely friendly and helpful, verbal directions can cause confusion that is truly disconcerting, even disorienting. Though it sounds vague, it is actually fairly simple.

"Up to" or "up from" - north - "We was up to Logan (a city in northern Utah)."

"Down to" or "down from" - south - "He come down from Logan to visit."

"Over to" or "over from" means either east or west, especially short distances - "He went over to the mall" but not if he's south of it, though, for then "He goes up to" or "down to" the mall (which may also mean the mall is on a hill).

"Out to" means one of two things 1) far away east or west "He went out to California." It also connotes a rural passage, though it may be relatively close. "She took him out to see the farm." You can tell how far away a person lives from a lake or how far out on the lake people have gone if they say that someone went "out to the lake" instead of "over to the lake."

And one more little lesson before an example. There is an interesting lexicon reserved almost entirely for the female population. I call it "Relief Society" Utahnics. It is apparently a way of sounding diminutive, feminine, or cute:

"Dist" - just
"Bit" - but
"Ginna" also "Gidda" - going to, as in, "I'm gidda go git the mel."
"Everbiddy" - everybody
"Enybiddy" - anybody
"Simbiddy" - somebody
"Nobiddy" - nobody
"Rully" - really
"Gyud" - good
"Noyss" - nice

Now let's use the foregoing to decipher this typical conversation:

"Hiya, LaDawn . . ."
"Fine."
"Dja hear bout DeVerl's campout?"
"No, where dee go?"
"Ee went out rilly close to the Still Mell."

"Up to Geneva, did ee?"

"Yep. Ee dist took ees sleepeen beg and pellow, went over there with tin of ees mell students down there, dist for fun."

"How spacial! Bu'. . . ees so conservateev, I never woulda took him to do sometheen that librel!"

"Irrigardless, ee wint dist fer playsure!"

"Playsure, geoll, who zee think ee is, anyways?"

"Ats right. Ees gotees nerve alright."

"That's air boy, DeVerl, fer you!"

One of the major tendencies of Utahnics is to convert either the "oh" or "ooh" sounds. These "o" sounds may be replaced by the short "a" sound:

"Praise the Lard" - Praise the Lord
"Harse" - horse
"Carn" - corn
"Cargated" - corrugated
"Gearge" - george
"Garge" - gorge
"Marmon" - as in Book of Mormon
"Shart" - short
"Carthouse" - courthouse
"Farce" - for us
"Dar" - door
"Farce" - force (this is tricky, see above)

One not so rare variant is the "Panguitch dialect." In addition to the above, speakers also substitute the forbidden "o" sound for the "a" sound as in "barn in a born" (born in a barn).

"Barn" - born
"Force" - farce (and see above)
"Worn" - warn
"Warn" - worn
"Sharn" - shorn
"Yorn" - yarn

"Tarn" - torn
"Fart" - fort
"Fort" - xxxx
"Chorge" - charge

A famous example: "Darthy, that's a gargeous ahrnge farmal! You'll be a rill farce tonight."- Dorothy, that's a gorgeous orange formal! You'll be a real force tonight.

Another example: "We was down to the carthouse when that shart dar got blocked. Air lawyer, ee used considerble farce and farced the dar farce."

And finally, no explanation of Utahnics would be complete without a short discussion of expletives. Since cussing, profanity, and swearing are frowned upon by the dominant religion, an entire lexicon of expletives has been invented to cover invective (invecteev). "Dang," "heck," "shoot," and "gosh," are all used liberally. Though golly is rarely used, a version has survived as a female expletive.

"Shoot" - mild
"Dangit" - mild
"Goshdangit" medium
"Goshdangitalltuheck"- dramatic
"Keyrud" - crud - mostly male expletive
"Flip" - mainly a male expletive as in "What the flip is that?!"
"Flippeen" - an expletive as in "What does ee flippeen think ee's doeen?"
"Fetch" or "fetcheen" - an expletive, used the same as flip
"Freak" or "freakeen" - an expletive, (see above)
"Geeeall" - a female expletive (the goll as in golly)

"Fer ignernt" - a female expletive NOTE: "fer" can be placed in front of any noun to make an expletive, i.e. "Fer rude, Fer stupid, Fer cute(que*), Fer neat(nee*)."

"Eeeuuuuu" - a female expletive reserved for registering disgust or horror

"Dist shir" - Just sure

"Dist so shir" - Highly sarcastic female expletive

"Ohmyheck" "Ohmygosh" or "Ohmycrud"- expletives used to signal discovery or surprise

"Ohmyflippeenkeyrud!" a young man might say if he suddenly discovered his zipper was down while he attempted a speech to his peers.

You are now "acauainted" with Utahnics. Equipped with this knowledge, let's see if you can translate and understand this exchange between LaMont and Earlene on their date. They are sitting at a table in a pizza shop when their conversation becomes animated:

LaMont: Flip, Earleene, ya don't have to take and git so uhmoshnal about this!

Earlene: (loudly through tears) I'm dist so shir, LaMont, Ohmyheck, I can't even bleev I'm sitteen here listneen to this!

LaMont: Keyrud, Earlene, djew know whatcher sayeen? Yore be'een completely unrelisteek!

Earlene: I'm unrelisteek?! I'm unrealisteek? Fer ignert, Lamont. I'm warn out with worneen you! Ohmyheck, I have tried everytheen.

LaMont: Goshdangit, Earlene, will you keep yer flippeen voice down?! This is embarrasseen!

Earlene: Ohmygosh, ohmycrud, you frekin think yer embarrassed? I never relized what a fanateek you are. Probly everbiddy whose enybiddy knows bit me! Its probly the favert topeec of conversation.

LaMont: Crud, Earlene, I don't see the uhmergency. Djew know whatcher talkeen about? Djew know what dar yer opneen? Djew have iny idea what kinda force yer makeen in front of all these people?!

114

Earlene: That is so lame, Lamont. Geeall! You can be such a bu*head sometimes! I guess you think yer be-een rully que* . . .

(She gets up and makes for the door.)

LaMont: Goshdangitalltoheck, yer makeen me crazy. (He jumps up after her, turning the table over.) Oh flip! Freakeen fantasteek!!! Fetcheen brilliant!

Earlene: Rully gyud, Lamont, Fer nea*!

Lamont: I guess you be'een sarcasteek is exposta make me sorry.

Earlene: Eeeeeuuuuu! Fer rude. Fer rude and crude!

Lamont: I don't have to take this garbeedge. I'm going down to Spanish (Fork) and you can just find your own flippen way home.

Earlene: Fer cool! I wun't ride'th you feye had to. Now you know how I been feeleen all this time!

Conclusion: Though this is only a beginning primer you'll find it invaluable in "Marmon" society. Don't worry, you probly be fine and everbiddy's langueedge will be an open dar to knowleedge.

Left to right; Aunt Minnie June, Heber, Tiffany, Leroy, Viola

Family Songs

There is nothing in the world so uplifting as to lift up your voices in song with those of your own gene pool. (Expecially if they can carry a note.) This being the case we have prevailed upon Verdell every year to furnish us with family songs we can sing together roundst the campfire, or roundst gramma Phoebe's old piano, or roundst the Christmas Tree or roundst . . . well, anything you can get roundst of!

These here is not all we got, no sir (and some ain't worthy of print anywho! If you know what I mean), but as I was saying, these here is some of our very moist favorites. And we won't even sue you if you use them, too. So just insert your own family name where it says to and raise your voices high. (Once we had the police called on us but that was because it was real late at night, not our singing . . . at least, that's what they said.)

* Put in your fam'ly name.

©Lisa Farley   Fam'ly Reunion Song #1

Ev'ry bo-dy come to the ✱ re-u-nion Don't let me here you moan,

Meet those mem-bers E-ven in sus pen ders And then we'll all go home.

Come meat your Grand pas, Come meat your Grand mas COME AND PAY YOUR DUES!!

Eat some food It will put you in the mood And hear some fam'ly news.

We are the best the best in the west the east the south the North—

Let's hear some noise for the ✱ girls and boys for their the best FOR SHORE.

✱ Insert family name

119

© Lisa Farley 1998   If You Have a Fam'ly (Song #2)

F ... If you have a fam'ly have a re-u-nion **C7** Their a

C7 lot of fun for each and ev'ry one. **F** Since re-

Bb u-nions are such fun They can take a-way the glum **F** Their a-

C7 lot more fun than cut-ting **F** on-i-ons!!!

2nd verse: The ** ** reunion is the best.
Their smarter than the rest.
* bigger
better
older   * (only pick 3)
smaller
faster
quicker

* *put in
your fam'ly
120 name

From their head down to there toes
Our fam'ly really grows
The ** ** fam'ly really stands the test.

© Lisa Farley 1998 — At Our Reunion (Song #3)

At our re-u- nion, which will be out doors, The fam 'lies
wait - ing for you and yours. Jel- lo, pie and beans
Oth -er fan- cy things Will be there just a wai-tin' for you, That's
where you'll want to be At our re- u- nion which will be out doors...
(start over)

This is a song that never ends!

Right to left: Uffer K. Johnson, Saucy Ulbrecht, Nephi J., Mahonri Dean, who was all declared equal winners in the watermelon eating contest.

The 10 Most Important Things to Avoid at Your Family Reunion

In all my years at the family reunion, I seen a lot of things. Believe you me. There was some things, though, I wish I hadn'ta. Here's a list of things that will definately reck your reunion (for sure) and should be avoided at all costs:

#10. Letting the kids dry off the cat, parakeet, puppy, or guinea pig in the new microwave oven.

#9. Using a hairnet as an emergency food strainer. (Which I actually seen tried before—and put a stop too.)

10 Most Important Things to Avoid

#8. Using raw gasoline to goose the lighting of the charcoal brickettes for the Barbieque.

#7. Posting of a public list of them who should NOT eat the bean cassaroll.

#6. Saying ignernt things to each other, such as: "Are those real?" [or, patting someone's tummy], "Whens it due?" or [after just getting there standing up to say], "Well, I guess that about wraps it up," or [holding up the box and shouting], "Who's box of Depends are these?"

#5. Bouncing a check for your dang outstanding dues.

#4. Bringing your Amway presentation kit.

#3. Pointing out strong odors or stains on people when you don't know what made them.

#2. Drinking from ANY paper cup, glass, or container that's got standing liquid in it.

And the number one most important thing to avoid at your family reunion

#1. Failing to show up!

THE FONDEST OF FARETHEEWELLS

Ohmygosh, Ohmyheck! I've did it! I have wrote it all down for you. Now that is a cherishing thought. Talk about amazing. I have to say that I never really knew I had so much to say. Its enough to choke a horse. But on the other hand its been like how cheese is: the more aged it is the more expensive it is.

Nobody hose the row alone and I am exspecially grateful for the companions and helpers I have had along the way. And without naming names I know that you know who they are.

Sometimes I just sit and wonder how it is that I been so lucky (or blessed) to have come to such a great family. Oh, I know there is those that thinks that our family (the Farleys) is pretty strange. Its pretty hard to admit, but there was a time when even Aunt Pearl thought the same. That was till I got my eyes yanked wide open. (Yes, we got our inlaws, but that come later.) You see, from my work down to the genealogical library I can say this generation of Farleys don't have no lock and key on strange—it was pretty well handed down to us and our kids (for instance their was our ancestor who was his own grampa . . . TRUE! Now THATS strange!).

But, in fact, after I seen the way things is done out there in the world at large, how families fall apart and hate each other, throwing things and one another, suing and countersuing onto each other before judges and juries and featuring all kinds of nasty, wicked, and worldly behavior I had to ask myself what is more strange—People who spend all their time in unrightious dominions and tearing away at each other (as demonstrated regularly on TV talk shows) or people with probly a few little quirks who love each other and, by dang, show up for each other once a year out to the family reunion? Well, there ain't no contest to my way of thinking!

Our family is about people who love each other. In most cases the more stranger they is the more love they has poured down upon them. I will not go onto naming of names, but there is those in our family who wouldn't stand a candy bars chance in a boy scout troop of making it on their own. And look at them now! Not to tear the family down but to say, "Hey, lookee what the Lord done over here! He put someone in our care who maybe no one else would care about." And ain't we grateful?! I don't know about your family, but I feel the Farleys is handpicked for greatness. Not in the worldly sense, of coarse. (I ain't nieeve even

Heber and friend take a "cat nap"

though I been accused of it a couple a times.) I say, what's the big deal with nieeveness, anyhow? Look at my age, look at my kids, look at my grandkids, and see if you don't think I got it made in the shade with lemonaid!

No, nobody in the Farleys is going to be very rich (although there's a couple got some money, for what that's worth and see what happened there) and nobody's probly going to rise to be President of these United States or a famous movie star type. But the way they run their lives I can only say, "Thank the Lord. I think I'll just stick with them Farleys, thank you very much." Thats the place where I can make my difference. Thats the place where they love me in spite of me. And thats the place where I rose to significance in my earthly labors however insignificant those labors might look to others. But really, significance is in the eye of the beholder, don't you think? So when others looks upon and judges our family as insignificant, I say, "You ain't seen nothing yet!" Better search for that beam of yours before crossing my mote.

So, the next time you look around and think you've got it pretty tough, look a little farther and you'll see that things ain't so bad afterall. Why I even know people who draw strength for theirselves by looking at the Farleys. Who's problems would you like to trade with, anyways? Those you don't even know about, or those your sitting on right now?

Thanks all you Farleys down through the ages. Thanks for finding me a place on this old planet under your family roof. I see as I look around me lots of places I'd just as soon not go live, and people I'd just as soon not be related to (although I sometimes wished I had their recipes).

I look at the Farleys, my Farleys, like an old overstuffed sofa. We are definately not the kind people you'd be afraid to sit on for fear of dirt, or the kind that looks great but sits like a concrete slab. Our people is the big old soft kind that you can let your kids crawl over forever, washes up after messes, and you can jump onto and take a nap on even with your shoes on! Now that's creature comforts! (I been called "sentimental" by some for this outlook which I got, but I tell you I'd rather be sentimental anyday than the reverse!)

So how did we get that way? Well, if you gotta ask then you ain't been reading, it come directly through the family reunion is one of the ways. When your knee to knee and nose to nose with the jean pool as produced you, there's something there to be learned if you'll only open up your baby blues (or browns or whatever) and take a look around. You start thinking, "My heck! This here's my family, this here's my kissin kin, I'm supposed to learn something here." Whether you learn to ride a bike, set a jello salad, sew your shirt, or just weather the storm, its all with people you was somehow meant to be with.

I will end this part of my book with Heber's favorite saying (that he overheard weigh back when he was in the Tabernacle Choir, before it got so infamous) that has been repeated so often in this family that we all know it by heart now. It is simple but really meaningful for us Farleys, as we are pretty simple as well.

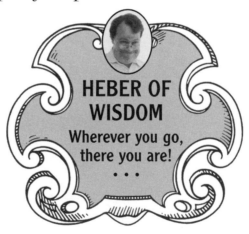

HEBER OF WISDOM
Wherever you go, there you are!
• • •

Now there's a statement for the ages. Contemplate the length and depth and breath of that!

Well, kids, its been fun. I taught you all I could think of regarding

Family Reunions. It only now revolves upon you, (and each and every one of you) to go out and put your rear in gear and put the petal to the medal. You now know the tricks of the trade from one of the trickiest in the trade. NOW, BLESS YER HEARTS, GO OUT AND DO LIKEWISE, I'M SURE.

BESTEST OF LUCK, Yours,

Pearl!